Guide to implementation of phytosanitary standards in forestry

FAO
FORESTRY
PAPER

164

FOOD AND AGRICULTURE ORGANIZATION OF THE UNITED NATIONS
Rome, 2011

The designations employed and the presentation of material in this
information product do not imply the expression of any opinion whatsoever
on the part of the Food and Agriculture Organization of the United Nations
(FAO) concerning the legal or development status of any country, territory, city
or area or of its authorities, or concerning the delimitation of its frontiers or
boundaries. The mention of specific companies or products of manufacturers,
whether or not these have been patented, does not imply that these have
been endorsed or recommended by FAO in preference to others of a similar
nature that are not mentioned.

ISBN 978-92-5-106785-7

Text in this guide is not an official legal interpretation of the International Plant
Protection Convention (IPPC) or its related documents, and is produced for
public information and guidance only.

Contents

Figures

Boxes

Foreword

New threats to forest health from insects, pathogens and other non-indigenous pests are emerging due to growing global trade and the exploitation of new market opportunities. Habitat modification and increased international pest movements associated with the trade of plants, plant products and other articles such as containers, soil, industrial equipment and personal baggage have all contributed to the spread of pests both within and between countries. Management of pests and preventing their spread plays a key role in helping ensure forests remain healthy, meeting sustainable forestry objectives.

National plant protection organizations (NPPOs), designated under the International Plant Protection Convention (IPPC), have historically dealt mostly with agricultural crops. In recent years, however, forest pests have become a more prominent concern and increased communication between forest sector personnel and the NPPOs is needed. All sectors in forestry need to understand what the IPPC is, and how NPPOs work so that the forest sector can play its part in implementing International Standards for Phytosanitary Measures (ISPMs) and help preserve forest health. Understanding the content of ISPMs, which target phytosanitary experts, is not always easy for foresters and differences in phytosanitary and forestry terminology often needs explanation.

FAO therefore initiated a multistakeholder activity to prepare this guide to provide the forest sector with clear and concise guidance on forest health practices, including plain language descriptions of the ISPMs and suggestions for their improved national implementation. The guide has been prepared through a consultative process involving an international group of scientists, phytosanitary authorities and forest sector representatives and is supported by the IPPC Secretariat at FAO.

Understanding and implementing the ISPMs is vital in maintaining forest health and vitality, particularly with expanded global trade increasing the risk of new pest introductions and factors such as local climatic change increasing the possibility of establishment of pests in new areas. This guide will help develop this understanding and assist policy-makers, planners and managers to improve communication between agencies at a national level and apply these standards in the forest sector.

Jose Antonio Prado
Director, Forest Assessment, Management and Conservation Division
FAO Forestry Department

Acknowledgements

FAO has produced this publication with financial support from the FAO-Finland Forestry Programme "Sustainable forest management in a changing climate" and in collaboration with an international group of scientists, phytosanitary authorities and forest sector representatives, and extends sincere thanks to all the group's members and their organizations for their dedication and time.

Gillian Allard (FAO), Kerry Britton (USDA-Forest Service) and Beverly Moore (consultant) coordinated the development of the publication with text drafted by and input from:

- Hesham A. Abuelnaga, International Trade Specialist, Africa, Middle East and Russia, Office of Scientific and Technical Affairs, Foreign Agricultural Service USDA, United States of America
- Eric Allen, Research Scientist, Pacific Forestry Centre, Natural Resources Canada, Canada
- Roddie Burgess, Head of Plant Health Service, Forestry Commission, United Kingdom
- Hugh F. Evans, Head, Forest Research Wales, United Kingdom
- Edson Tadeu Iede, Forestry Researcher, Centro Nacional de Pesquisa de Florestas, Empresa Brasileira de Pesquisa Agropecuária (Embrapa), Brazil
- Su See Lee, Head, Forest Health and Conservation Programme, Forest Research Institute Malaysia (FRIM) and Vice President, IUFRO, Malaysia
- Keng-Yeang Lum, Chief Scientist, CABI Southeast and East Asia Regional Centre, Malaysia
- Sarah Ahono H. Olembo, Technical Advisor, Sanitary and Phytosanitary Standards and Food Safety, African Union Commission, Ethiopia
- Andrei Orlinski, Scientific Officer, European and Mediterranean Plant Protection Organisation (EPPO), France
- Shiroma Sathyapala, Team Manager, Plants Imports and Exports Group, Border Standards Directorate, Ministry of Agriculture and Forestry, New Zealand
- Shane Sela, Standard Setting, IPPC Secretariat, FAO, Italy
- Adnan Uzunovic, Research Scientist – Mycologist, FPInnovations, Canada
- Brian Zak, Phytosanitary and Market Access Specialist, Canada Wood Group, Canada

Thanks also to members of the IPPC Secretariat, in particular, Brent Larson, Standards Officer, and Ana Peralta, Implementation Officer.

Thanks are extended to the USDA Foreign Agricultural Service Office of Scientific and Technical Affairs/Plant Division and to the European Plant Protection Organization (EPPO) for translation of this guide into Arabic and Russian, respectively.

Many thanks are extended to those who assisted with the preparation or review of the publication including:

Albania: Kristaq Nicaj, Ministry of Agriculture, Food and Consumer Protection

Argentina: Juan C. Corley, INTA EEA Bariloche; Vicky Paula Klasmer, Instituto Nacional de Tecnologia Agropecuaria (INTA); Raúl Villaverde, Secretaría de Agricultura, Ganadería, Pesca y Alimentos (SAGPyA)

Australia: Cheryl Grgurinovic, Biosecurity Australia; Simon Lawson, Queensland Department of Primary Industries; Glynn Maynard, Department of Agriculture, Fisheries, Forestry

Belgium: Marc Michielsen, CHEP

Bhutan: Dhan B. Dhital, Ministry of Agriculture and Forests

Bosnia and Herzegovina: Sabaheta Cutuk, BiH Ministry of Foreign Trade and Economic Relations; Tarik Trestic, University of Sarajevo

Brazil: Leonardo Rodrigues Barbosa, Camilla Fediuk de Castro and Susete do Rocio Chiarello Penteado, Empresa Brasileira de Pesquisa Agropecuária (Embrapa); Carlos José Mendes, Parana State Association of Forestry Companies

Canada: Pierre Bernier, Roxanne Comeau and Jacques Régnière, Natural Resources Canada; Colette Breuil, University of British Columbia; John Huey, Sundance Forest Industries

Chile: Aida Baldini Urrutia, Corporacion Nacional Forestal (CONAF)

China: Xu Fuyuan, Forestry Academy of Jiangsu Province; Luo Youqing, Beijing Forestry University; Wang Yuejin, Chinese Academy of Inspection and Quarantine Science

Colombia: Olga Patricia Pinzon F., Universidad Distrital Francisco Jose de Caldas

Denmark: Hans Peter Ravn, University of Copenhagen

Fiji: Viliami Fakava, Secretariat of the Pacific Community

Germany: Thomas Schroeder, Julius Kühn-Institute, Federal Research Centre for Cultivated Plants

India: Nitin Kulkarni, Tropical Forest Research Institute

Indonesia: Sri Rahayu, Gadjah Mada University

Italy: Davide Paradiso, Consorzio Servizi Legno-Sughero

Japan: Kazuyoshi Futai, Kyoto University; Yuji Kitahara and Motoi Sakamura, Ministry of Agriculture, Forestry and Fisheries (MAFF); Hayato Masuya and Takeshi Toma, Forestry and Forest Products Research Institute; Yuichi Yamaoka, University of Tsukuba

Kyrgyzstan: Almaz Orozumbekov, Kyrgyz National Agrarian University

Lithuania: Vaclovas Kucinskas, State Plant Protection Service of Lithuania

Malaysia: Laurence G. Kirton, Forest Research Institute Malaysia (FRIM)

Netherlands: Nico M. Horn, Ministry of Agriculture, Nature and Food Quality

New Zealand: Eckehard Brockerhoff and Lindsay Bulman, Scion; Bill Dyck, Bill Dyck Ltd; Gordon Hosking, Hosking Forestry Ltd; Allanah Irvine and Shane Olsen, Ministry of Agriculture and Forestry

Philippines: Marcial C. Amaro, Jr., Ecosystems Research and Development Bureau

Russian Federation: Oleg Kulinich, All-Russian Center of Plant Quarantine

Seychelles: Samuel Brutus, Ministry of Environment and Natural Resources

Slovenia: Jošt Jakša, Slovenia Forest Service; Dusan Jurc, Slovenian Forestry Institute

South Africa: Solomon Gebeyehu, USDA-Foreign Agricultural Service; Michael J. Wingfield, University of Pretoria

Spain: Gerardo Sanchez, Direccion General del Medio Natural y Politica Forestal

Sri Lanka: Upul Subasinghe, University of Sri Jayewardenepura

Sudan: Nafisa H. Baldo, Agricultural Research Corporation

Switzerland: Daniel Rigling, Swiss Federal Research Institute WSL

The Former Yugoslav Republic of Macedonia: Kiril Sotirovski, University "Sv. Kiril i Metodij"

Timor-Leste: Manuel da Silva, Ministry of Agriculture

Trinidad and Tobago: Mario Fortune, Ministry of Agriculture, Land and Marine Resources

Uganda: James Epila-Otara and Peter Kiwuso, National Agricultural Research Organisation

Ukraine: Valentyna Meshkova, Ukrainian Research Institute of Forestry and Forest Melioration

United Kingdom: Andrew Gaunt, Food and Environment Research Agency; Andy Gordon, European Forest Nursery Association; Andrew Leslie, University of Cumbria; Ian Wright, National Trust

United Republic of Tanzania: Ismail K. Aloo, Forest and Beekeeping Division

United States of America: Fred Ascherl, Rio Tinto Minerals; Marilyn Buford, Phil Cannon, Robert A. Haack, Andrew M. Liebhold, Michael L. McManus, Carlos Rodriguez-Franco, Noel F. Schneeberger, Borys M. Tkacz and Shira Yoffe, USDA-Forest Service; Bruce Britton, University of Georgia; Faith Campbell, The Nature Conservancy; William Ciesla, Forest Health Management International; Edgar Deomano, National Wooden Pallet and Container Association (NWPCA); Peyton Ferrier, USDA-Economics Research Service; Deborah Fravel, USDA-Agricultural Research Service

Uruguay: Ines Ares, Ministry of Livestock Agriculture and Fisheries (MGAP); Nora Telechea, Consultant

CABI: Matthew Cock and Marc Kenis, CABI Europe, Switzerland; Roger Day, CABI Africa, Kenya

European Commission: Robert Baayen and Ana Suarez Meyer, Belgium; Lars Christoffersen and Bernd Winkler, Ireland

International Institute of Tropical Agriculture (IITA): Danny Coyne, United Republic of Tanzania

FAO: Khaled Alrouechdi, Graciela Andrade, Jim Carle, Roberto Cenciarelli, Arvydas Lebedys, Joachim Lorbach, Felice Padovani, Andrea Perlis and Maria Ruiz-Villar, Rome; Jorge Meza, FAO Representation, Paraguay; Alemayehu Refera, Subregional Office for Eastern Africa, Ethiopia; Mohamed Saket, Regional Office for the Near East, Egypt

Acronyms

CBD	Convention on Biological Diversity
CPM	Commission on Phytosanitary Measures
CITES	Convention on International Trade in Endangered Species of Wild Fauna and Flora
IFQRG	International Forestry Quarantine Research Group
IPM	integrated pest management
IPPC	International Plant Protection Convention
ISPMs	International Standards for Phytosanitary Measures
IUFRO	International Union of Forest Research Organizations
NPPO	national plant protection organization
PFA	pest free area
PFPP	pest free place of production
PRA	pest risk analysis
RPPO	regional plant protection organization
SPS	WTO Agreement on the Application of Sanitary and Phytosanitary Measures
TPFQ	Technical Panel on Forest Quarantine
WPM	wood packaging materials
WTO	World Trade Organization

1. Introduction

It is very important to protect the world's forests from harm. The global forest area is just over 4 billion hectares, which represents 31 percent of the total land area (FAO, 2010a). Forests are important global resources that provide a wide range of environmental, economic and social benefits. They provide a variety of valuable products, such as timber, fuelwood, fibre and other wood and non-wood forest products, and contribute to the livelihoods of rural communities. They provide vital ecosystem services, such as combating desertification, protecting watersheds, regulating climate, and maintaining biodiversity, and play an important role in preserving social and cultural values.

Forests can also play a significant role in addressing global climate change concerns. For example, they absorb carbon from the atmosphere and store it in trees and forest products. Properly managed forests can also provide wood, a renewable alternative to fossil fuels. Conserving overall forest area, replanting harvested forests, and managing forests to maintain vigorous growth are all important ways to reduce carbon dioxide accumulation in the atmosphere.

1.1 PEST THREATS TO THE WORLD'S FORESTS

The health and vitality of the world's forest ecosystems are affected by a range of natural disturbance agents including pests,[1] drought and fire. While disturbance is part of the natural succession processes in forests, it can often limit the ability to meet forest management objectives. A wide range of pests can have negative impacts on forests and the forest sector. Outbreaks of forest insects alone damage some 35 million hectares of forests annually, primarily in the temperate and boreal zones (FAO, 2010a).

Indigenous pest species may become a significant problem, particularly when they reach outbreak populations on introduced tree species. Sometimes even more damage is caused by non-indigenous or introduced pests, which have been accidentally introduced through trade in forest products, live plants and other commodities. Since non-indigenous pests did not evolve with the forests they are affecting, their impacts can sometimes be devastating. In such situations, introduced pests may not have natural enemies that normally keep populations in balance. The new host trees may have insufficient or no resistance to introduced pests. Climate change also appears to be influencing pest establishment in new locations, as well as increasing the severity of impacts of both indigenous and non-indigenous pests. Examples of major pest introductions and their impacts on forests can be found in Annex 1.

---

[1] Any species, strain or biotype of plant, animal or pathogenic agent injurious to plants or plant products (ISPM No. 05, 2010, *Glossary of phytosanitary terms*).

1.2 PROTECTING THE WORLD'S FORESTS

Successful protection of the world's plants, including forest tree species, from pests requires coordinated international action. This coordination occurs through the International Plant Protection Convention (IPPC), which is an international agreement between countries to control pests and prevent their spread. The IPPC's governing body is the Commission on Phytosanitary Measures (CPM), which adopts International Standards for Phytosanitary Measures (ISPMs)[2] to prevent pest introduction and spread and facilitate trade. As of December 2010, 176 countries are contracting parties (members) to the Convention. Under the guidance of the IPPC, most governments have designated national organizations to protect natural resources, including forests, from pest entry and establishment. These are collectively referred to as national plant protection organizations (NPPOs)[3] although countries may call them plant health inspectorates, quarantine services or many other names. NPPOs frequently have to work with neighbouring countries to prevent pest entry and spread between countries. This collaboration may be through regional plant protection organizations (RPPOs).

NPPOs are the official national points of contact to the IPPC, and it is the NPPOs that work together to develop ISPMs. All member countries unanimously agree that ISPMs are effective in managing pest risks and allowing safer trade. NPPOs use the ISPMs as the basis for their national phytosanitary regulations. Because they will have an impact on trade, it is important for everyone involved in forest products trade to understand how these regulations can affect them. ISPMs developed by the IPPC are recognized by the World Trade Organization (WTO), which provides a dispute resolution process for trade issues.

1.3 ABOUT THIS GUIDE

Many people associated with the forest sector can play a key role in preventing the spread of pests, including those involved in growing, planting, managing, harvesting, manufacturing, storing, trading and transporting forest products. This guide is intended to help reduce human-facilitated pest spread and its impacts. It provides easy-to-understand information on ISPMs and the role of forest management practices in implementing phytosanitary standards and facilitating safe trade. Specifically it explains:

- how the ISPMs and NPPO regulations affect the import and export of forest commodities (Chapter 2);
- how people in the forest sector can reduce the risks of spreading pests through effective management approaches (Chapter 3);
- how ISPMs can be used to prevent forest pest introduction and spread (Chapter 4);
- how forest sector personnel can work together with NPPOs to contribute to the development and implementation of ISPMs and national phytosanitary

---

[2] The titles of all existing ISPMs, and a short summary, are given in Annex 3.
[3] The full list of NPPOs and their official contact persons can be found on the IPPC Web site: www.ippc.int.

regulations that help reduce pest movement while being as least restrictive to trade as possible (Chapter 5).

Each chapter has been prepared as a stand alone document allowing the reader to concentrate on the specific topics that are of interest. A glossary is also provided to further clarify the terminology used.

This guide will be of vital interest to all sectors in forestry and will also benefit forestry policy-makers, planners, managers and educators, particularly in developing countries.

2. Trade in forest commodities

The volume of wood products in international trade increased 125 percent between 1992 and 2008 (FAO, 2010b). Some examples of the changes in volume of exports of particular commodities are given in Figure 1. Many countries want to promote international trade in forest commodities, but also recognize the importance of protecting plants, including forests, from pests.[4] National plant protection organizations (NPPOs)[5] should implement International Standards for Phytosanitary Measures (ISPMs)[6] as part of their national phytosanitary regulations for imported forest commodities. NPPOs also certify, where required, that export consignments meet the phytosanitary import requirements of other countries.

Import requirements for the same commodity may differ from country to country. Usually these differences are the result of variations in countries' assessment of the pest risks associated with the commodity. These variations can be due to differences in forest susceptibility to pests or in the levels of pest risk which the countries accept

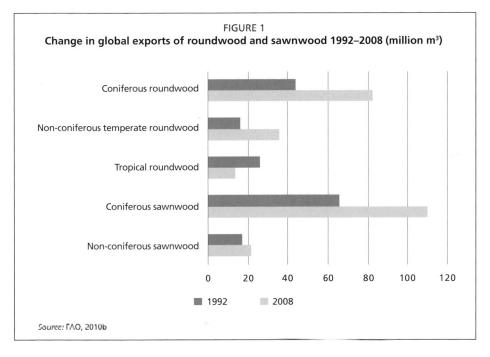

FIGURE 1
Change in global exports of roundwood and sawnwood 1992–2008 (million m³)

Source: FAO, 2010b

---

[4] Any species, strain or biotype of plant, animal or pathogenic agent injurious to plants or plant products (ISPM No. 05, 2010).
[5] The full list of NPPOs and their official contact persons can be found on the IPPC Web site: www.ippc.int
[6] The titles of all existing ISPMs, and a short summary, are given in Annex 3.

(see Box 1). New ISPMs are currently being developed (see Chapter 5) to assist with the import and export of forest commodities, and to reduce pest spread.

This chapter explains some aspects of how ISPMs and NPPO regulations affect the import and export of forest commodities under world trade agreements. Since import and export are closely linked, it is recommended that Sections 2.2 and 2.3 be read together.

BOX 1

Logs: an example of the relationship between pest risk and phytosanitary import requirements

While wood may contain many kinds of organisms, not all logs pose the same level of risk of movement, establishment and spread of forest pests. Countries may vary in their assessment of the risk associated with the import of logs depending on the area of origin, the tree species and size, the presence or absence of bark, or whether the pest(s) of concern are present and widely distributed in the country in question. Some countries do not have any phytosanitary import requirements for logs; some require phytosanitary certification based only upon visual inspection for pests. Other countries may require or accept a particular treatment and in some cases certification that treatment has been undertaken prior to export. These phytosanitary import requirements are established based upon the assessed risk of pests moving on or in the logs.

For example, logs moving from tropical countries to Canada, a temperate country, might contain pests, but these will be geographically constrained, i.e. restricted to tropical climates and trees. Because Canada has no tropical forests, it also has few phytosanitary import requirements for tropical species. However, if these same logs contained pests that could establish and cause damage to important plants in the importing country, the NPPO may prescribe specific phytosanitary measures prior to export to manage this risk.

Logs – high risk commodity?
Perceptions differ

A. UZUNOVIC

2.1 FOREST COMMODITIES

Forest commodities are wood and non-wood products produced from plants and trees grown in forests or other wooded lands. Because of the wide range in the quality of wood and in the processes used to create forest commodities, the risk of pest infestation and the measures that can be used to manage that risk vary with different commodity types. Some examples of commodities ranked from higher to lower risk are given in Box 2. Further details on opportunities to reduce pest risk in forest commodities are given in Chapter 3.

BOX 2
Forest commodities, their pest risks and risk management options

Plants for planting, excluding seeds
Plants for planting (nursery stock including bonsai and rooted Christmas trees) are increasingly recognized as carriers of pests, which could be associated with stem (wood and/or bark), branches, foliage, fruits/cones, roots and sometimes soil or growing media. Bonsai plants, potted Christmas trees and large trees for planting present higher risks as they have most of these plant parts. A variety of pests may move with plants for planting, including: aphids, scale insects, adelgids, bark beetles, weevils and moths; nematodes; foliar, seed, cone, root-rot and canker fungi; pathogenic oomycetes; and bacteria, viruses, viroids and phytoplasmas.

Importing countries generally conduct a pest risk analysis (see Section 4.2) to identify pests of concern and ways to reduce the risks.

Pest management measures that may be applied include surveillance, pest-specific surveys, identification of pest-free areas, treatments, pre-shipment inspections, and post-entry quarantine or prohibition, among others. Additional opportunities to inspect for pests could occur during handling plants for planting (including pruning, harvesting and packaging) by appropriately trained personnel.

Cut branches
Cut branches, including Christmas trees without roots, may carry many of the same pests as plants for planting but the risk of pest transmission to living host trees is less because they are most often used indoors. This limits their pest risk to natural environments. However, when they are discarded they may contain insects that are strong fliers or rust spores which may be easily spread by air currents and rain splash.

Christmas trees are a widely used commodity and are often grown as a monoculture which increases the potential for pest outbreaks and spread. These trees are often moved during a limited portion of the year and if properly discarded may not present a risk for pest movement.

Pest management measures that may be applied include pest surveys, harvesting from pest-free areas, treatments, pre-shipment inspections, safeguarded disposal after use, or prohibition, among others.

continues

Roundwood/logs (related names: poles, posts, timber, pilings)

Roundwood with bark is considered higher risk than roundwood that is debarked or bark-free. Both commodities can carry pests, however debarked wood is less likely to have pests that colonize bark or the portion of wood immediately below the bark.

To manage insect pests living in or just under the bark of logs, bark removal, heat treatment or fumigation is generally used. For deep wood-boring insects, heat treatment or fumigation is the primary pest management measure. Irradiation could also be used where applicable. For fungal pathogens, fumigation, heat treatment and end-use processing can reduce pest risk. Visual inspection during post-harvest grading helps to selectively remove infected logs, although in some cases it is not sufficient to identify early stages of decay.

Fumigants only penetrate a portion of the outer surface of the logs, and are considered less effective on logs with bark, particularly with wet bark.

Sawnwood (related names: boards, lumber, timber, squared wood)

Sawnwood has less risk than roundwood because sawing removes most of the bark as well as some of the outer wood thus eliminating most wood pests living in or just under the bark.

The risk management measures suggested for roundwood are equally effective for sawnwood. The risk of infestation by blue-stain fungi and some wilt organisms may be managed by reducing the moisture content of the wood, e.g. kiln-drying.

Wood chips

The risk from wood chips depends on their size and especially on how the chips will be stored and used. Wood chips used as landscape materials could spread small insects, nematodes or fungi. Where wood chips are used for pulp production or energy generation, the processing will kill the pests. But poor conditions during transport, storage and handling prior to use may still present a risk.

The smaller the wood chips, the lower the risk of most insect pests, however chipping may not lower the risk of pathogens surviving. Pest risk can be managed by heat treatment, moisture reduction of the chips, fumigation, and safeguarding during transport and storage.

Fuelwood

Fuelwood is often produced from low quality wood or from trees infested with various pests (i.e. bark beetles, deep wood-boring insects or fungi). Consequently, the transportation of fuelwood both domestically and internationally often spreads pests. In-country transport of fuelwood, which is often unregulated, is an efficient pathway for the spread of introduced species once they have become established in localized areas.

Heat treatment or fumigation as well as proper safeguarding during transport and storage could reduce pest risk.

Bark

Bark can carry a number of pests (e.g. insects, fungi, nematodes). Bark may be used for fuel, as landscape mulch, as a growing medium, or to produce processed wood products. Pest risk depends much on the intended use. Infested bark used as mulch or growing media presents the highest risk.

Some of the measures to manage pest risk include: heat treatment, irradiation, moisture reduction, fumigation, composting, safeguarding during transport and storage, and prohibition.

Wood packaging materials

Wood packaging is sometimes made from low quality boards that may contain pests, either in the wood or associated with bark remnants. These have been internationally recognized as high risk.

Therefore the packaging materials must be made from debarked wood (with specified tolerance), heat treated or fumigated, and marked with a specific internationally accepted mark (see Section 4.3).

Wood-based panels

Wood-based panels, such as veneer sheets, plywood, particleboard (including oriented strand board) and fibreboard (including medium density fibreboard), are assembled with the use of heat, pressure and glue and are generally free of primary wood pests. Check with your NPPO to see if newer processes that use cold temperatures, environmentally friendly glues and pressure are acceptable as a phytosanitary treatment.

Termites or dry wood borers can infest almost any wood products after manufacture, even if heated. Inspection can be used to detect infestations.

Manufactured wood products

Manufactured wood products, such as handicrafts and furniture, are diverse and their risk is dependent on the origin of the wood, the species of wood, the degree of processing and the intended use. If the processing methods used are not likely to kill pests, further treatment, such as heat treatment, fumigation or irradiation, may be needed.

Forest seeds

Seeds can carry pests either on the surface or internally. The degree of pest risk depends on the seed pest type, origin of the seed, pest detection reliability, and storage conditions in the place of the end use.

Some of the measures to manage pest risk include: monitoring at the place of origin, recognition of pest-free areas, and seed testing for pest detection. If infestation of seeds is detected, appropriate measures, such as destruction, heat, chemicals or irradiation, could be needed or the export should not be performed.

High risk commodities such as nursery stock often need to be accompanied by a phytosanitary certificate

ISPMs and national regulations apply to any item that may be infested or contaminated by pests. These regulations also apply to any organism that can serve as a vector, or could be a potential pest itself. Regulated articles may also include any equipment used to process or transport goods. Examples of such articles include logging trucks, wood handling equipment, shipping containers, barges, ships, railway cars, wood packaging materials and other storage units that are necessary to move forest commodities.

2.2 IMPORT OF FOREST COMMODITIES

Contracting parties – countries that are members of the IPPC – have the sovereign right to make regulations to protect their resources, including forests, from the introduction and establishment of pests. For pests of concern, each country's NPPO may establish regulations that specify their phytosanitary import requirements for commodities through the use of an evaluation process called a pest risk analysis (PRA, see Section 4.2). Forest sector personnel can play an important role in assisting the NPPO to determine pest status and keep regulations up-to-date and effective by sharing pest information, supporting survey activities for pests, and providing information about new pests.

NPPOs of importing countries establish phytosanitary import requirements based on an evaluation process that carefully considers all aspects of a pest's risk, including:
- its biology and association with the commodity;
- its potential to be moved in association with the trade of commodities;
- its potential to enter, establish and spread in the importing country;

- its potential to cause economic and/or environmental harm if it becomes established and the resulting consequences.

This process, commonly referred to as a PRA (see Section 4.2), requires an evaluation of the existing scientific evidence and technical information and may take several years to complete. Simple PRAs which take less time and resources may still afford a good understanding of the risks and enable trade with the application of appropriate pest management measures.

Once the PRA is complete, the importing country may establish regulations and appropriate phytosanitary import requirements to manage the risk or prohibit the import of a consignment from a specified origin. Import requirements are decided by the importing country's NPPO, but can often be negotiated bilaterally between the NPPOs of importing and exporting countries. Import requirements may include activities to be carried out in the exporting country, in transit, or upon entry to the importing country (Box 3). Industry must comply with import

---

BOX 3

Examples of phytosanitary measures that may be applied to forest commodities

Prior to export
- Assurance that the commodity originates from an area or a place of production that is free of specified pests
- Commodity production based on specific requirements (e.g. debarking)
- Inspection during growing season and prior to shipment
- Appropriate treatment or post-harvest handling
- Prohibition of imports

During transport
- Phytosanitary treatments (e.g. in-transit fumigations, chemical sprays)
- Safeguarding (covering or enclosing the commodity in containment)
- Transport within a specified period (e.g. Christmas trees may only be shipped during pest dormancy)
- Restrictions on transport through or storage in pest-free areas

After arrival in the importing country
- Inspection
- Processing in a particular way
- Entry and use within a specified period or season
- Post-entry treatment
- Post-entry quarantine

This is not an exhaustive list and many of these examples may be used singly or applied in combination to manage a single pest or group of pests.

and export requirements, so importers wishing to import forest commodities should initially contact the nearest office of their NPPO.

Imported consignments of forest commodities, especially those considered high risk (e.g. nursery stock, seeds, untreated roundwood with bark or Christmas trees), are often required to be accompanied by a phytosanitary certificate which is issued by the NPPO of the exporting country (see Section 4.10). A phytosanitary certificate is a document certifying the health of the plants, plant products or commodities, or confirming treatment. It is a written statement that the consignment is compliant with, or meets, the importing country's requirements. It certifies that any measures that are required to be taken prior to export have been satisfactorily completed or that appropriate provision has been made for any measures to be applied during transport.

Commodities that fail to meet the phytosanitary import requirements may be treated at the point of entry, rejected from entry to the importing country, destroyed, redirected to another country that will accept them, or returned to the exporting country. When consignments are rejected because they fail to meet the import requirements, NPPOs should notify the exporting country so that corrective actions may be taken to avoid repeat rejections (see Section 4.11). Rejected consignments may result in significant costs to both the importer and the exporter.

Most countries make special arrangements to permit the entry of normally prohibited articles for academic or industrial testing, some limited industrial applications, or for small quantities of imports. These arrangements are usually developed on a case by case basis and are determined by the NPPO of the importing country. Usually the NPPO of the importing country provides a special written permit (import permit) or letter to authorize this type of limited import. Figure 2 shows the steps that may be followed to import or export forest commodities.

2.3 EXPORT OF FOREST COMMODITIES

To export forest commodities, the exporter should first contact its NPPO. NPPOs have cooperative relationships with the NPPOs of countries with which they trade. Ideally, the exporting country's NPPO should have information about the phytosanitary import requirements of different countries and the steps that need to be followed in order to export goods. The exporter may also obtain details about requirements directly from the importing country's NPPO, or through the importer, who can obtain the requirements from its NPPO. Exporters should be aware that different countries may have different requirements for a commodity, even if those different countries appear to be geographically related. It is in the best interest of exporters to ensure that commodities comply with requirements prior to export.

If the importing country has not developed specific phytosanitary import requirements for a particular commodity there may be a need to initiate a PRA, as shown in Figure 2. For that PRA, the NPPO of the importing country may request

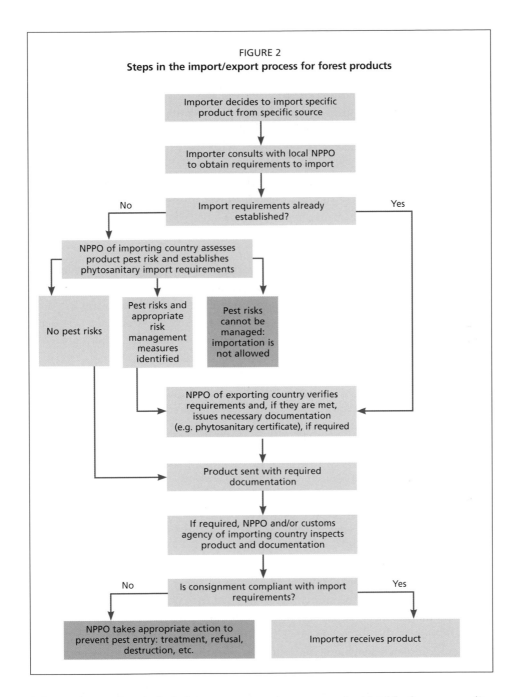

FIGURE 2
Steps in the import/export process for forest products

information and technical data on potential pests associated with the commodity from the NPPO of the exporting country and may even request a description of potential measures that could be applied to manage the risk of pest movement.

Often the NPPO of the exporting country has more information about the forest pest issues associated with the commodity, and can cooperate with the importing country's NPPO. This cooperative process between NPPOs may aid in the possible development of bilateral arrangements that can establish specific import requirements for a commodity from a specific region. These arrangements may also provide a mechanism for deciding whether to permit normally prohibited or regulated items to enter for scientific or industrial testing, with an alternative phytosanitary measure.

For many imported forest commodities, a phytosanitary certificate is required, which must be issued by the NPPO of the exporting country. The NPPO of the exporting country makes arrangements with the exporter to verify that the import requirements (i.e. treatments, production practices) have been met and to conduct any required inspections. Some activities required in support of phytosanitary certificates, such as periodic inspections during the production cycle and integrated pest management activities, may be more effectively carried out by foresters, under the NPPO authority, during the handling and processing of harvested wood (see Chapter 3).

The NPPO of the exporting country may conduct inspections or it may delegate them to an authorized organization or individual under the NPPO's control and responsibility. In some cases, where commodities move from one country to a second country and then to a third country, a re-export phytosanitary certificate may be issued by the NPPO in the second country to meet the requirements of the final destination country (see Section 4.10).

Under bilateral agreements, other certificates, such as treatment certificates or manufacturer's declarations, are sometimes used as an alternative, or in addition to, the phytosanitary certificate. These certificates often contain only a portion of the information required on a phytosanitary certificate, such as when, where and how a specific treatment was applied.

NPPOs of some countries require an import permit which specifies their phytosanitary import requirements and authorizes the importation of the commodity. Usually, the importer is responsible for obtaining an import permit and providing the details to the NPPO of the exporting country through the exporter.

Certain processed forest commodities (e.g. plywood, fibreboard) are recognized to pose less pest risk, and so may be exempted from certain requirements. The NPPO may require certification of the kind of processing completed for the product that qualifies for these exemptions. Some general guidance to NPPOs is available on the types of forestry commodities that may not require a phytosanitary certificate as a result of processing and the intended use.[7]

In addition to the phytosanitary regulations of an importing country, there may be other requirements including those arising from the Convention on International Trade in Endangered Species of Wild Fauna and Flora (CITES), the Convention on Biological Diversity (CBD) and other international agreements. In some cases, these separate requirements may be administered by an authority other than the NPPO. Some exporting countries may also require permits for the export of viable materials, such as those with potential to provide useful medicinal drugs.

---

[7] Annex 1 of ISPM No. 32 (2009), *Categorization of commodities*, provides guidance on the risks associated with certain processed commodities.

Trucks loaded with logs and semi-processed wood are transported by ferry in Brazil

In addition to forest products themselves, equipment used to harvest or transport forest commodities may pose a risk for the movement of forest pests. Increasingly NPPOs are establishing import requirements for the entry of such equipment. Containers and other storage units could also be contaminated with pests, soil or forest commodity waste (i.e. branches, leaves, plant debris). These should be cleaned after use and the contaminant materials disposed of in a manner that effectively manages risks such as burning, deep burial, or reprocessing into other commodities. Note that in some countries, local environmental or waste management regulations may influence decisions on how material may be treated or disposed of. The relevant authority should be consulted before proceeding.

3. Good practices for forest health protection

Forests are ecosystems that are composed of all forms of life. Insects and micro-organisms live in and on trees, exploiting their leaves, bark, wood and roots for shelter and food. Forest products are therefore likely to contain these organisms at any time. Many species that are considered pests[8] in some importing countries may not be considered pests in their native range. Thus, while it is obvious that a forest that is undergoing a disease or insect outbreak poses a more immediate threat to international trade, products from a healthy forest may also pose a pest risk. Nevertheless, good forest health should be a minimum aim of sound commercial forest management. Keeping forests healthy requires careful planning throughout all of the resource management phases from planting or regeneration to harvest. Harvest planning should include careful consideration of what will likely grow back and how the next generation of forest will be managed. This chapter provides basic information on integrated pest management (IPM) as well as pest management practices for all of the phases of, and sites involved in, forest resource management, including:

- forest operations: planning, harvest and transportation;
- forest nurseries;
- planted forests;
- naturally regenerated forests;
- post-harvest treatments and sawmills;
- product transportation and distribution.

Many of the suggested practices, such as sanitation, surveillance, and quick reporting to the national plant protection organization (NPPO),[9] are applicable and good for all phases of forest management. These management options can be selected and adapted to individual conditions. It should be noted that, in some countries and in some situations, it may not be possible to implement all of these best practices, particularly after natural disasters and unexpected events which may create economic constraints and the need for immediate actions such as salvage.

3.1 INTEGRATED PEST MANAGEMENT FOR FORESTRY

The most effective way to deal with forest pests is integrated pest management (IPM). IPM can be defined as a combination of prevention, observation and suppression measures that can be ecologically and economically efficient and socially

---

[8] Any species, strain or biotype of plant, animal or pathogenic agent injurious to plants or plant products (ISPM No. 05, 2010).

[9] The full list of NPPOs and their official contact persons can be found on the IPPC Web site: www.ippc.int.

Release of Pauesia *parasitoids for biocontrol of cypress aphid,* Cinara cupressivora, *in western Kenya*

acceptable, in order to maintain pest populations at a suitable level. Prevention may include proper tree, variety and site selection, natural regeneration, and planting and thinning practices that reduce pest populations and favour sustainable control by natural enemies. Careful monitoring of pest populations, for example through visual inspection or trapping systems, determines when control activities are needed. For suppression, mechanical control, biological control through the use of natural enemies and biopesticides, or other sustainable control methods are preferred over synthetic pesticides. IPM relies on understanding the biology of the tree, forest and pest as well as the biology of natural control agents that can help keep pests under control. Therefore, for IPM to be effective, field staff must be trained to recognize pests, monitor population levels and use biological control agents and other suitable control methods.

Biological control through the use of natural enemies is an essential component of IPM. Beneficial natural enemies may be promoted by suitable silvicultural practices (biological control by conservation) or by supplemental releases (biological control by augmentation), the latter including also the use of biological pesticides, based on microbial diseases of pests and weeds. A third approach commonly used in forestry, classical biological control, consists of controlling non-indigenous pests and weeds by importing natural enemies (parasitoids or predators or pathogens for pests; arthropod herbivores and phytopathogens for weeds) from their country of origin. This approach has been carried out successfully for well over a century. However, over the years, practitioners have become increasingly aware that introduced biological control agents may have undesirable side-effects.

Initially, this concern was limited to the possible impact of these introduced agents on economically important plants and insects (notably honey bees, silk moths and weed biological control agents). More recently, increased environmental awareness has drawn attention to the potential danger to all indigenous fauna and flora, particularly rare and endangered species. ISPM No. 03 provides guidelines for the safe use of exotic natural enemies in biological control programmes. When considering biological control agents, it is vitally important to have information on the pest (its identification, importance and known natural enemies), the natural enemy (identification, biology, host specificity, hazards to non-target hosts, natural enemies and possible contaminants, and procedures for their elimination), and human and animal health and safety issues. Ultimately the decision whether to use a biological control agent may depend on economics and science-based estimates of the likely results of biological control agent introduction versus the economic and environmental costs of other control options, such as pesticides, or doing nothing and accepting the losses due to the pest.

3.2 FOREST OPERATIONS

Forest operations personnel can minimize pest movement through careful operational planning, harvesting, wood storage and transport (see also Section 3.8). The movement of pests from the harvest location to the processing site can be prevented during timber marking and harvesting, particularly when wood volume and quality are evaluated. Personnel should be trained to recognize and report unusual pests and symptoms of diseased or infested trees, and to perform practices that reduce the risk of pest populations moving to other locations.

Debarking infested logs can help avoid the spread pests from the harvesting site to the processing site; here workers remove bark from logs infested with the southern pine beetle, Dendroctonus frontalis, *in Belize*

Minimizing pest population levels during harvest and processing will reduce the incidence of pests in the commodity prior to export and make transport easier and safer. This is particularly important if the harvested wood is to be moved internationally. In addition, potential impacts of phytosanitary measures on trade can be reduced by identifying and reporting uncommon pests to the NPPO, particularly if the pest is detected early and can be eradicated (see Section 4.6). Box 4 offers more specific guidance on operational practices that reduce pest presence.

Phytosanitary considerations are particularly critical when targeting international markets. These considerations need to be balanced against other important forest resource management decisions such as meeting biodiversity goals, recreational uses and fire suppression. Economics and local regulations are also important factors in forest operations decision-making.

BOX 4
Planning and operational practices that minimize pest presence in forests

- Select the appropriate genotype of trees for the site. If the trees are not well suited to the soil or climate then they will become weakened and susceptible to attack by insects and pathogens.
- Identify any pest outbreaks during the field planning phases and report these to a pest professional. If relevant, report them to the NPPO or other regulatory authority. Species that are not considered pests in one country may be considered pests in another.
- In addition to recording all pest outbreaks, record where the pests occur. This will assist in determining pest free areas in the future.
- Conduct systematic surveys designed to detect and assess increases in levels of forest insects and pathogens and their resultant damage. Report unusual pest occurrences to forest managers, NPPOs, forest landowners and other stakeholders in a timely manner.
- Use knowledge of pest development biology and weather events to predict pest emergence and choose an optimal time to apply control measures to prevent outbreaks.
- Consider harvesting those stands with a high incidence of dead and dying trees to prevent more loss of stock by damage and to reduce the risk of pest spread. Extract and burn dead trees on site or use locally to avoid the spread of pests to other areas.
- Consider layout of harvest boundaries to reduce the chance that trees remaining after the harvest might blow down and provide food for pest build-up.
- Prevent erosion and subsequent weakening of trees which can make them more susceptible to pests, through harvesting practices appropriate to the landscape.
- Avoid damage to standing trees during forest operations as this can affect vigour, enable infection by wood-degrading fungi, and increase susceptibility to other pests.

- Remove felled trees from the forest quickly to avoid a build-up or an outbreak of pests.
- When felled trees have to be stored near or in the forest, consider removing the bark. This will help avoid spreading pests such as some wood borers and bark beetles.
- Transport logs during the dormancy period of known pests and apply appropriate control measures at the final destination before the pests emerge.
- When moving or storing wood originating from natural disturbances such as wind storms and fire, ensure operations do not allow the spread of pests.
- Where appropriate, store wood under cover, under water sprinkler systems or in ponds, and install pheromone or light traps to reduce further infestation or outbreaks spreading to surrounding areas.
- Properly dispose of, or manage, debris from harvesting, thinning and pruning to ensure that associated pests are not spread to other areas.*
- Sanitize equipment and transport containers to avoid transfer of pests.
- Permit harvesting of branches for commercial purposes (including Christmas trees or tree parts) only in areas that are not infested with pests
- Provide training to foresters, forest landowners and other stakeholders on how to recognize key pest species and their damage and on the procedures for reporting pest occurrence.

---

* In some countries, local environmental or waste management regulations may influence decisions on how material may be treated or disposed. Check with the relevant authority before proceeding.

3.3 FOREST NURSERIES

Since each forest nursery can supply plants for planting to many geographic areas, keeping pests out of nurseries is especially important. Buying healthy stock and carefully monitoring the condition of seedlings and cuttings are important practices. If possible, keep new plant materials separate from the main growing area for a period of observation, to prevent bringing pests into the nursery. Forest nurseries use intensive management practices which, if not properly done, may promote pest build-up. The artificial environment of the nursery, such as planting density, species or clone choice, and monoculture, can be favourable to pest development.

To minimize damage, detecting and treating pests before they spread is essential. Operational procedures should require that any workers who see symptoms of pests that are unknown in the nursery must report immediately to their manager. Nursery managers should notify the NPPO or other appropriate officials if an unknown organism or an important or regulated pest is found. Further guidance on good nursery practices is provided in Box 5.

If forest nursery plants are intended for international trade, it is necessary to follow the importing country's phytosanitary requirements. A phytosanitary certificate may be required to certify to the NPPO of the importing country that the consignment has been inspected and found free of regulated pests and that it fulfils the phytosanitary import requirements (see Section 4.10).

BOX 5
Good nursery management practices that minimize pest presence

- Provide the best possible growth conditions (e.g. nutrients, water, light, appropriate spacing and weed control) to raise healthy, vigorous and resistant plants.
- Collect or obtain seed from good quality genetically superior trees; use multiple sources of planting material to increase genetic diversity; use certified seed if possible and store seed in conditions that limit pest attack; test seed prior to planting to ensure good germination and seed health; and apply seed treatments, if needed. If possible determine pest resistance to the main pests in the country; multiply and distribute the resistant stock.
- Locate the nursery producing the seedlings away from commercial stands to prevent contamination and the subsequent spread of pests around the country. Keep new plant material isolated from main growing areas, where it can be monitored for pests without risk of them spreading to the whole nursery.
- Keep appropriate records that permit identification of sources of production material, and where it is grown and planted out, so that the source of any infestation/infection may be traced.
- Use soil or an inert growing medium that is free from insects, pathogens and weed seeds.
- Treat soil if necessary to kill pests before planting.
- Establish monitoring systems to permit the early detection of pests. Use adhesive traps to detect the presence of insect pests and spore traps to detect fungal spores.
- Take immediate action if pests are detected.
- Use appropriate preventative silvicultural, chemical or biological control methods.
- Ensure irrigation water is free of pathogens and other contaminants such as pesticides, particularly if the water source is a pond where water accumulates from infected or treated fields or is suspected to be contaminated. Simple filtration systems can be installed to sanitize infested water.
- Avoid leaving leaves wet, especially when watering at night, as this can allow pathogens to infect plants. Trickle irrigation rather than sprinklers can help keep leaves dry.
- Install screens or nets in plant production facilities to prevent insect entry or spread.

- Inspect materials prior to transport to ensure plants are free of pests.
- Nursery managers should notify the NPPO or other appropriate officials if an unknown, important or regulated pest is found.
- Rotate crops to avoid recurring pest problems; make sure the alternative crop is not susceptible.
- In infested areas, limit the entry of visitors to reduce the risk of pests and pathogens moving on their clothing and footwear. Measures to limit the entry of animals and birds, which may spread pests, should also be considered.
- Clean (thoroughly remove all soil and plant materials from all surfaces and crevices) and, if necessary, disinfect all tools, footwear and equipment before entering and before leaving the nursery area, especially if a pathogen is present. Clean and disinfect tools that are used for different operations within the nursery before and after use.
- Dispose of infested soil or growing media carefully so as not to contaminate new plants or soil.
- Collect and remove dead plants and debris every week to decrease the probability of infestation. Destroy or sanitize infested plant waste by burning, composting or treating with heat to kill the pest. If composting, make sure that a high enough temperature is reached to kill the pest.
- Use deep burial (2 m) to dispose of plant waste that cannot be destroyed or sanitized by other means.*

---

* In some countries, local environmental or waste management regulations may influence decisions on how material may be treated or disposed. Check with the relevant authority before proceeding.

FAO/FO-7038/J. CARLE

Forest nursery, Angola

3.4 PLANTED FORESTS

Some of the nursery IPM practices are also useful in managing planted forests. Forest health problems can be prevented by using appropriate genetic material that meets provenance (geographic origin) and species requirements, or the appropriate size and type of seedlings or cuttings. Choosing the most suitable species for the site's soil and climatic conditions reduces plant stress, and thus susceptibility to infestation by pests. Understanding local pest status can also help avoid placing susceptible species into conditions that favour the pest.

Field surveys, including evaluation of forest health condition, can help with early detection of any new pest introductions, and ensure prompt action. Surveys are also needed to make sure that seedlings will be free of competition from weeds. Control of weeds may help promote tree growth and facilitate silvicultural activities. However, the potential for negative effects of weed control, such as soil erosion and reductions in biodiversity, should be considered. Further guidance on planting practices is provided in Box 6.

Diseases, insect pests and weeds can be spread from one location to another during the movement of site preparation equipment and routine silvicultural activities, such as pruning and thinning. Proper cleaning and sanitizing of equipment is therefore important. Equipment, tools, footwear and vehicle tyres should be cleaned of soil and organic matter before spraying with a disinfectant, such as industrial alcohol, when working in areas infected with diseases of quarantine significance. Flame sterilization can be used for some kinds of tools. If none of these are available, vigorous washing with steam or soap, if available, will reduce risk.

Planting a diversity of species or block planting of species in planted forests can help reduce susceptibility to forest pests; trees planted in this forest in Viet Nam are a combination of pine and acacia

BOX 6
Good planting practices that minimize pest presence

- Be aware that monocultures and clonal plantations can be more vulnerable to pests than mixed forests.
- Avoid reliance on a single tree species or clone.
- Choose the correct provenances (geographic origin) and tree species appropriate to the site and climate to ensure strong and healthy plants.
- Select appropriate growing sites to ensure healthy plants and avoid future pest problems.
- Consider the potential of the species to become a pest when selecting non-indigenous tree species for planting.
- Be cautious when moving plants with soil; if possible use bare rooted plants.
- Move bare root plants when dormant and less likely to spread forest pests. This also reduces plant stress. The potential of termite attack should be taken into consideration when planting bare root crops.
- Provide healthy growing conditions, with sufficient water, sunlight and nutrients to avoid stress.
- Provide adequate spacing between field-planted seedlings to reduce susceptibility to pests.
- Consider appropriate cultural practices to allow for good drainage and root expansion and breathing.
- Clean and disinfect footwear and equipment (e.g. tools, vehicles) before entering and before going off-site, particularly if the site is infested, to help reduce the spread of diseases such as root rot. Disinfect tools after each use.
- Survey often, particularly after planting, to ensure forest management goals are met and to ensure pests are not prevalent.
- Control weeds to ensure that crop plants are able to grow well. Consider encouraging weeds that promote natural enemies of pests without harming trees.
- Where silvicultural wastes from pruning and thinning can be a breeding substrate for pests, dispose of them properly by burning, deep burial, composting or heat treatment sufficient to kill pests.*
- Notify the NPPO or other appropriate officials if an unknown organism or an important or regulated pest is found.

---

* In some countries, local environmental or waste management regulations may influence decisions on how material may be treated or disposed. Check with the relevant authority before proceeding.

As planted forests mature, activities such as spacing, pruning, thinning and fertilization may be practiced depending upon available resources and management objectives. Forest managers must be ever vigilant to preserve and enhance forest health during these management activities.

Agroforestry systems, where trees are integrated into farms and agricultural landscapes, pose a complicated situation for pest management considerations. Pests can sometimes spread between agricultural crops and trees. The crop or tree can act as host for a given pest or as trap crop. Extra care must be taken when harvesting non-wood forest products particularly fruits and nuts to ensure that diseases are not transmitted through wounds caused by harvesting techniques.

3.5 NATURALLY REGENERATED FORESTS

Forests can be naturally regenerated by the sprouting of roots or stumps from the previous harvest, or natural seeding. In some forested areas, understory plants that are present prior to harvesting may help fill-in the natural seeding process. However foresters need to work for several years prior to harvest to ensure that these existing plants, called "advance regeneration", are present and vigorous. In some cases natural regeneration is more resilient to environmental stresses because the species are well adapted for the site and they can be more vigorous. Using natural regeneration also reduces the likelihood of introducing new pests with plants for planting.

Even when using natural regeneration, the reforestation of any site requires planning and follow-through. In some cases, specific management and harvest practices can be selected to promote natural regeneration and minimize the impacts on the ecosystem. Surveys of the advance regeneration will be needed to ensure that these plants are undamaged and healthy enough to compete with weeds and become part of the new forest.

FAO/FO-7027/H. BATUHAN GUNSEN

Natural Pinus sylvestris *forest with regeneration, Turkey*

It is important that natural seeding be adequate to meet long-term management objectives, based on tree species and stocking requirements. To ensure that healthy trees are established, monitoring and pest surveys in the appropriate follow-up time frame are necessary.

Later, monitoring and pest surveys will be necessary to determine whether or not the natural regeneration is sufficiently free from weeds or competition from understory plants. Competition may also come from root-suckering of some deciduous species or overstocking by natural seeding of certain conifers.

During silvicultural activities such as density control, pruning and fertilization it is imperative to ensure that these activities and the associated equipment and tools do not move pests or intensify their impacts (see Box 7).

BOX 7
Good practices for naturally regenerated forests that minimize pest presence

- Choose the most appropriate regeneration process, or combination of processes, to ensure healthy and vigorous forests.
- Conduct pest surveys to determine the probability of success of the natural regeneration process.
- Choose the most appropriate silvicultural, pest protection and harvesting practices to promote regeneration and reduce pest populations in the future forest.
- Conduct follow-up surveys to verify that regeneration is successful and to check for pests.
- Ensure appropriate spacing between naturally regenerated plants to reduce susceptibility to pests of concern and to promote tree growth.
- Control weeds when and where appropriate, giving due consideration to their potential beneficial effects of natural enemies of pests.
- Properly dispose of silvicultural wastes from pruning and thinning where they can be a breeding substrate for pests.*
- Perform activities, such as pruning, thinning and harvesting of non-wood forest products (i.e. chestnuts, resin, sap and branches), during periods of low risk so that wounds do not allow the entry of pathogens.
- Clean and disinfect footwear and equipment (e.g. tools, trucks) before going off-site, particularly if site is infested, to help reduce the possibility of spreading diseases such as root rot. Disinfect operational tools after each use.
- Notify the NPPO or other appropriate officials if an unknown organism or an important or regulated pest is found.

---

* In some countries, local environmental or waste management regulations may influence decisions on how material may be treated or disposed. Check with the relevant authority before proceeding.

3.6 SAWMILLS AND POST-HARVEST TREATMENTS

Following harvest and transportation of the forest products to the sawmill, it is important to process the roundwood promptly and carefully to reduce existing pest populations and minimize opportunities for pests to attack the wood. Debarking logs can be helpful if sawing will not occur promptly. The range of post-harvest treatments is wide. Treated commodities for export should be kept isolated to minimize the risk of post-treatment infestation.

All roundwood should be visually examined on arrival at the sawmill for signs of insects and disease. Ideally, those who provide logs should alert the sawmill operator about any potential pest problems. These should be investigated and reported to the NPPO or other appropriate authority if the pest is unusual or not known. An important determinant of whether pests can spread from stored forest products to forests is the proximity of the storage site to forest.

Even when it is planned to move the harvested trees during the pests' dormant period, seasonal weather patterns may change the timing of pest emergence. Some action in the storage area (either in the forest or at the sawmill) may therefore be necessary, such as placement of pest traps or application of cover sprays. For example, the cut surfaces of oak roundwood intended for production of valuable wood-based panels such as veneers are treated with wax to prevent oxidation and to reduce humidity. Some sawmills sprinkle water on log piles or submerge logs in ponds to reduce bark beetle attack until the wood can be processed. Pest forecasts can also be developed to predict when pests are likely to emerge and spread. These can be elegant models based on host and pest development biology and climate data, or simple systems based on previous experience. For example, following a mild winter more bark beetles survive which may lead to increased damage or faster spread. Local technical experts can advise sawmill operators if there are practical solutions for the types of insects and pathogens likely to be present locally.

Ensuring that vehicles and other equipment used to transport wood from the forest to the sawmill are cleaned of bark, plant debris and soil immediately after unloading is good practice and will substantially reduce the risk of accidental spread of pests. If infested wood is transported then it is better to use covered, enclosed trucks if possible to minimize the risk of pest escape.

Bark and other residual products should be gathered and stored securely for further utilization or safe disposal. It is quite common for pests to be present in residual or waste materials and these materials need to be properly managed to prevent pest infestations from occurring near the sawmill.

Processed wood and wood products should be monitored and graded to remove those products that show the presence of pests such as signs of fungi, insect holes and frass (debris or excrement). This quality grading step provides further assurance that the products being delivered or dispatched are less likely to create insect or disease outbreaks. Those products that have been removed because of the presence of a pest risk should be safeguarded and processed, or disposed of where it is safe to do so. Treatment to kill the pest, such as pasteurization by heat treatment, irradiation or fumigation, may be an option. Box 8 lists general good practices for sawmills.

Sorting wood in a sawmill, Canada

BOX 8
Good practices for sawmills and post-harvesting treatments to reduce pest spread

- Consider on-site treatment of freshly felled logs where practical.
- Examine harvested logs prior to entering the sawmill to determine if pests are present and might spread to surrounding products or areas.
- Logs with advanced decay should be set aside so that decayed sections can be removed and used or disposed of in a way that safeguards the remainder. This reduces the amount of visual examination in the production process.
- If new, important or regulated pests are discovered or if there appears to be a potential pest outbreak in the harvesting, manufacturing or storage areas, contact your NPPO or other regulatory authorities.
- If feasible, store log piles under cover, under water sprinkling systems, or in ponds to reduce existing or potential infestations. Pheromone or light traps, strategically and carefully placed to minimize pest spread, may be a part of the solution to reduce and control insect infestations.
- Transport infested loads in covered, enclosed trucks.
- Clean vehicles that transport logs and remove bark and debris for safe disposal immediately after unloading.

continues

- Continually gather up bark and debris from the storage yard for further utilization or disposal in a safe manner to prevent pest build-up and spread.*
- Monitor all products during the manufacturing process for the presence of disease or insect pest indicators. Separate infested products for safe utilization or disposal to prevent the movement, spread or introduction of pests elsewhere.
- Store infested products in a separate area to avoid contamination of pest-free products while in storage or awaiting transport or disposal.
- Post-harvesting treatments such as heat treatment, irradiation or fumigation may manage the risk of many pests. Contact your NPPO for further information on phytosanitary import requirements in the target market, and what treatments might be suitable for your products and the pests associated with them.

---

* In some countries, local environmental or waste management regulations may influence decisions on how material may be treated or disposed. Check with the relevant authority before proceeding.

3.7 PRODUCT TRANSPORTATION AND DISTRIBUTION CENTRES

The import and export of forest commodities relies heavily on seaports, temporary handling facilities, airports and train depots for the unloading and loading of containers and ships. Owing to the large number of forest commodities in movement and storage, these areas are critical in helping prevent the spread of pests.

To minimize pest contamination or infestation in ports, storage areas should be built on a hard or permanent surface (e.g. paving, concrete, gravel) and be free of vegetation, dead or dying trees, refuse and soil. It is important that the surrounding areas where export wood is stockpiled are kept free of pests.

To avoid cross-contamination, imported wood and wood for export should be stored separately with a suitably sized buffer zone between them. Similarly, treated and untreated wood should be separated. If there are places assigned for fumigation of wood, physical barriers should be constructed with insect-proof materials or covers to avoid recontamination of treated wood.

Potential pest infestation sources such as rejected logs, dunnage, broken wood pieces, or plant waste should be removed promptly and safely disposed of to avoid potential pest build-up.

Containers should be inspected prior to loading, to ensure that pests or soil and debris do not pose a pest risk. Container cleaning programmes using pressure washing or sanitation treatment may be necessary. Written procedures are needed to ensure worker safety and that phytosanitary goals are achieved.

Immediately prior to loading, it is also advisable to inspect forest products to ensure that they have not been infested while in storage. The record of this inspection can also serve as a monitoring record if pests are detected during inspection at the destination.

The proximity of transportation and distribution centres to forests greatly influences the probability that outgoing consignments can become infested with pests. Similarly, the proximity of forests to such centres influences the probability of successful pest establishment due to the availability of suitable habitat. Where product entry and exit facilities are located near forests it is useful to conduct surveys or other monitoring activities to detect establishment of new forest pests (see Section 4.6). In some cases, forests located near product entry and exit facilities may serve as sentinel or indicator plants. In addition, sentinel plants can be planted or located at points of entry such as ports and container terminals. With regular surveys they can help in the detection of any forest pests entering the country if they begin to exhibit signs of infestation. Monitoring tools, such as pheromone or light traps, and regular survey sites are recommended to help detect some insect pests, such as bark beetles. Traps are not effective against most wood borers, although trap logs can be effective for monitoring these pests, as well as some bark beetles.

There may be a need to protect consignments on conveyances from insects in those areas where insects, such as *Lymantria dispar* (gypsy moth, Asian subspecies in particular) and *Arhopalus ferus* (burnt pine longhorn beetle), are attracted to light. It is helpful to minimize the intensive lighting at ports and on vessels during periods of high risk and conduct loading operations and arrange departure times at periods of low insect activity. Pre-departure inspections or treatments of the commodity or conveyance may also be necessary.

By working with local scientists and national plant protection organizations, practical working solutions can be developed to improve pest management in the facilities engaged in the movement and distribution of forest products and thus protect forest health (see Box 9).

BOX 9

**Good practices for product transportation and distribution centres
to reduce pest spread**

- Build forest product storage areas on hard surfaces (e.g. paving, concrete, gravel, etc.) free of potential pest infestation sources such as soil and debris.
- Recycle or reuse off-loaded dunnage and wood packaging materials in consultation with the NPPO.
- Dispose of potential pest infestation sources such as waste from conveyances and broken products.*
- Implement standards and procedures for cleaning containers to ensure pests are not moved during the transportation process.
- Inspect products and remove infested wood prior to loading.
- Prevent cross-contamination between imported and exported products, and between treated and non-treated products.

continues

- Keep treated (ISPM No. 15) wood packaging materials separate from untreated wood packaging. Do not load treated wood onto untreated wood packaging materials.
- Implement monitoring programmes, including trapping, in those areas where entry and exit facilities are adjacent to forested areas, in collaboration with the NPPO.
- Promote awareness of pest infestations near seaports and develop systems to ensure conveyances and consignments are clean of hitch-hiker (contaminating) pests, including egg masses.
- Work with the NPPO to develop practical solutions for managing the risk of pest movement for facilities where the import and export of forest products are concentrated.

---

* In some countries, local environmental or waste management regulations may influence decisions on how material may be treated or disposed. Check with the relevant authority before proceeding.

3.8 USING A SYSTEMS APPROACH TO MANAGE PEST RISKS IN FORESTS

A systems approach in the regulatory world is the use of at least two independent risk management measures to reduce the risk of pests in order to meet import requirements. Foresters often apply many practices to reduce pest problems throughout the entire production process, from planting and managing forests to harvesting operations. These practices, often called integrated pest management (see Section 3.1), can help form the basis of a systems approach (see Section 4.5). Box 10 gives examples of pest management measures that foresters can use to reduce pest populations before products are sold and dispatched, and before associated pests pose a risk to forests abroad or affect profits at home.

3.9 CHALLENGES IN PREVENTING PEST SPREAD THROUGH WOODFUELS

The international woodfuel market is rather new, but appears to be growing as countries seek renewable energy sources to replace fossil fuels (Box 11). Woodfuel is a broad category that includes roundwood, wood residues, wood chips, wood pellets, fuelwood, charcoal and black liquor. Processed products present lower pest risks and pellets and charcoal, for example, need not be regulated.

Trees damaged by pests are frequently cut for fuelwood. Many of the pests that caused the tree to decline or die can survive in the wood for several years and be transported to new areas. Wood-boring beetles (e.g. *Agrilus planipennis* [emerald ash borer] and *Anoplophora glabripennis* [Asian longhorned beetle]) are the pests most frequently spread through this pathway, but *Sirex noctilio* (European woodwasp), termites and pathogens can also be transported on or in logs or branches.

It is becoming increasingly evident that even domestic movement of these commodities can cause undesirable spread of pests, and national regulations may be needed to prohibit movement from infested areas to pest-free areas, as China has adopted for the Asian longhorned beetle.

BOX 10
Examples of forest pest risk management measures that may be included in a systems approach

Before trees are planted
- Register seed and plant producers and provide training in proper handling methods
- Select appropriate genetic material
- Select healthy planting material
- Select resistant or less susceptible species or varieties
- Identify pest free areas, places or sites of production
- Consider ecological characteristics, such as soils, vegetation, biodiversity and other resource values, in planning and site selection and preparation

During growing seasons
- Perform inspections to detect pest presence
- Perform testing for diseases, e.g. root rot or *Phytophthora* spp.
- Reduce pest populations using practices such as disrupting pest breeding, preharvest treatments, biological control and pheromone trapping
- Reduce pest populations using appropriate silvicultural practices, such as sanitation to remove potential breeding substrates and avoid damaging crops during weed control, thinning, pruning, harvesting non-wood forest products and tree salvage
- Maintain surveys needed to certify low pest prevalence

At harvest
- Harvest trees at a specific stage of development or time of year to prevent the increase of pest populations
- Inspect and remove infested trees and logs
- Use sanitation practices, such as removing any waste that could be a potential breeding substrate for pests
- Use harvesting or handling techniques that minimize damage to trees and soil
- Remove felled wood quickly to avoid pest build-up
- Debark trees as soon as possible after felling
- Remove stumps or treat surfaces where necessary to reduce root rot or other pest problems
- Clean equipment between sites

Post-harvest treatment and handling
- Treat logs or other wood products to kill, sterilize or remove pests using heat, fumigation, irradiation, chemical treatment, washing, brushing or debarking
- Store logs or other wood products in ways that reduce pest buildup, such as under water

continues

- Inspect and grade logs and other wood products
- Use sanitation measures including removal of infested or infected parts of the host plant
- Sample and test forest products for pests
- Install insect screening in storage areas

In association with export and import
- Treat or process forest commodities to kill pests
- Apply phytosanitary restrictions on end use, distribution and points of entry
- Apply restrictions on the import season to avoid pest introduction
- Select appropriate method of packing, such as closed or covered containers, to prevent infestation or accidental escape of pests during transport
- Require post-entry quarantine of plants for planting to enable the detection of any latent infections
- Inspect and/or test forest commodities to verify pest status
- Use good sanitation practices for conveyances such as ships, containers and trucks

FAO/FO-5549/L. LE JEUNE

Even domestic movement of fuelwood can spread pests

BOX 11
Volume of woodfuels traded internationally (average 2001 and 2002)

Charcoal: 1 255 288 tonnes
Wood chips and particles: 26 742 650 m³
Fuelwood: 1 926 946 m³
Wood residues (wood waste): 6 282 628 m³

Source: Hillring and Trossero, 2006

Some countries have import regulations requiring heat treatment or fumigation to reduce pest risk on fuelwood. These requirements are easier to monitor and enforce in large commercial concerns, but small operations often lack this capacity. Enforcement of regulations on individuals moving fuelwood is next to impossible. Public education may be the best approach to reducing the spread of pests through fuelwood.

For international transportation, regulations for roundwood often apply to fuelwood. Treatments such as debarking or chipping can greatly reduce the survival of bark beetles, but heat treatment or fumigation provide better protection from pests, including fungal pathogens, that live deeper inside the wood.

3.10 CHALLENGES IN PREVENTING PEST SPREAD THROUGH PLANTS FOR PLANTING

Many forest pests are thought to have been introduced into new locations and hosts via plants for planting. Plants for planting may include roots, stem, branches and leaves, and sometimes even fruit, intended to be planted. With so many plant parts, they can potentially carry many diverse pests. Plants in growing media (unsterile soil) are generally considered higher risk. Pathogens are particularly hard to detect in plants for planting. Some examples of pathogens believed to be spread by plants for planting include: horse chestnut bleeding canker (*Pseudomonas*), ash dieback (*Chalara*), pitch canker (*Gibberella*), and several *Phytophthora* species including *P. ramorum*, *P. cinnamomi*, *P. alni*, *P. kernoviae*, *P. lateralis* and *P. pinifolia*.

There is little scientific literature on pests present on ornamental plants. Furthermore, scientists estimate that as few as 7 percent of the world's fungi are known to science. Some pathogens hybridize in the nursery environment, creating new organisms and adapting to new conditions and hosts. Special culturing methods and molecular tools, such as DNA sequencing (i.e. polymerase chain reaction [PCR]) and immunological detection (i.e. enzyme-linked immunosorbent assay kits [ELISA]), may be needed to confirm the presence of pathogens. These tools, and the time to use them, are rarely available to the inspectors assigned to monitor imported plant material. Undetected pathogens may spread via plants for

FAO/22117/R. MESSORI

Forest nursery, Egypt

planting and establish in natural ecosystems causing significant damage through spread to native and commercial plants.

The risk has been significantly increased by the rise in the volume of the ornamental plant trade as a result of shifts in global plant production. Owing to the huge volume of trade and the manner in which consignments are sent (typically tightly packed in containers), often only a small sample of the plant material is actually inspected (usually through visual inspection only). Current regulatory systems screen for regulated pests, but some pests are difficult to detect and some pests are not yet known. Some plants may look healthy but may contain latent or dormant pathogens.

It is therefore a huge pest management challenge to support the plant trade but at the same time to regulate pest spread and prevent potential devastating impacts on natural ecosystems. Possible solutions may include developing systems that attempt to reduce the incidence of pests on plants and in the surrounding environment throughout the production process. The European Union (EU), which at present comprises a single market of 27 member states without border controls, has introduced a "plant passport" system. The EU registers producers of high risk nursery stock and makes inspections to confirm the nursery is pest free, before authorizing the producer to issue "plant passports". The plant passport accompanies the plants to the final end user. This system enables regulatory personnel to track down the source of infested plants quickly and reduce pest spread within the EU territory.

Continuous updates of science databases, data sharing, and improved and updated inspection and diagnostic methods at various inspection points are also needed. In general, very efficient growing techniques to produce the healthiest plants are recommended. Additional measures may include efficient tracking of plant origin and voluntary or regulated exclusion of some types of the commodities at highest risk, e.g. large plants for planting with soil which are used to create instant woody landscapes. Education may be another tool to raise awareness of the potential danger and the global scale of the problem.

A new ISPM on integrated measures for managing pest risks associated with the international trade of plants for planting has been drafted within the IPPC and is in the review process.

3.11 CHALLENGES IN PREVENTING INTENTIONALLY INTRODUCED TREE SPECIES FROM BECOMING PESTS

Many non-indigenous plant and animal species that have been intentionally introduced into ecosystems outside their native range for their economic, environmental or social benefits have subsequently become serious pests. This problem is of considerable concern in the forest sector. Non-native tree species are often used in agroforestry, commercial forestry and desertification control. Many of these tree species are highly valued for their exceptional adaptability to a wide variety of sites, their rapid growth and the multiple uses of their products. However in some cases these same species have become serious threats to their ecosystems (Box 12). It is vital to ensure that such species serve the purposes for which they were introduced and do not become pests.

Careful pest risk assessment is recommended before introducing new plant species. The Australian Weed Risk Assessment (Pheloung *et al.*, 1999) has proven reasonably accurate over a broad range of ecological conditions (Gordon *et al.*, 2008) and is currently the most widely used system. For examples of the application of this assessment, see: www.weeds.org.au/riskassessment.htm.

FAO/CFU00342O/R FAIDUTTI

Many forest tree species, such as this young Acacia albida *in the Niger, are planted for the positive benefits and products they provide but have the potential to become invasive*

BOX 12
Examples of intentionally introduced tree species becoming pests

The forest sector often uses non-native tree species to provide a variety of benefits. Many of these have become major problems around the world.

- *Leucaena leucocephala* has been widely used as a source of wood, fuelwood, fodder and shade and to restore degraded lands, improve soils and stabilize sands. It is a fast-growing, nitrogen-fixing tree that is tolerant of arid conditions and saline soils and as such is highly regarded in arid regions in Africa and Asia. In areas where it has been introduced however, this species tends to form dense thickets and readily invades forest margins, roadsides, wastelands, riparian areas and agricultural lands (McNeely, 1999). Also, the toxicity of its seeds and foliage decreases its value as a source of fodder.

- *Prosopis juliflora* is very useful in controlling soil erosion, reducing the aridity of an area, and providing a source of fuelwood as well as fodder and shelter for both wild and domesticated animals. It has been introduced into many countries in Africa and Asia with some significant environmental and socio-economic impacts. This species displaces native flora resulting in reduced biodiversity and reduced diversity of products available to rural communities (McNeely, 1999). Its dense thickets also render invaded lands useless for agricultural purposes.

- Commercial tree species such as pine (*Pinus* spp.), eucalypt (*Eucalyptus* spp.) and rubber (*Hevea brasiliensis*) are important sources of wood and fibre and thus have been planted in many areas where they are not native. Several of these species have spread outside the areas in which they were planted with devastating impacts on ecosystems including reduced structural diversity, increased biomass, disruption of existing vegetation dynamics and altered nutrient cycling (Richardson, 1998).

- Many Australian *Acacia* species have been introduced into South Africa for timber and fuelwood as well as for tannins, which are used by leather industries, and for sand stabilization. Such species have radically altered habitats for wildlife resulting in major changes in the distribution of species, particularly birds. They have also altered nutrient cycling regimes in nutrient poor ecosystems due to their ability to fix atmospheric nitrogen (van Wilgen *et al.*, 2001). They have also decreased water supplies for nearby communities and increased fire hazards.

4. Phytosanitary concepts simplified

This chapter describes the International Plant Protection Convention (IPPC) and how the International Standards for Phytosanitary Measures (ISPMs)[10] are developed and adopted. Subsequent sections (4.2 to 4.12) describe the guidance contained in the standards that are particularly relevant to forestry and these are listed at the beginning of each of these sections. The standards help support good forestry practices and pest free trade, both in forest commodities and other commodities sent with wood packaging materials. For clarity, the descriptions assume ideal implementation of the standards and follow the IPPC definitions. In some cases, contracting parties (countries who are members of the IPPC) implement the standards differently. Implementation may be limited by scarce resources. Countries may also prescribe stricter phytosanitary import requirements, but they have to provide technical justification for doing so. The IPPC provides a dispute resolution process when countries file claims of unjustified trade restrictions.

4.1 THE INTERNATIONAL PLANT PROTECTION CONVENTION AND INTERNATIONAL PHYTOSANITARY STANDARDS

The IPPC Secretariat, hosted by the Food and Agriculture Organization of the United Nations (FAO), provides for close collaboration with related international organizations and conventions. The IPPC's governing body is the Commission on Phytosanitary Measures (CPM), which among other activities, adopts ISPMs to prevent pest introduction and spread and to facilitate trade. ISPMs are developed and approved through an international consultative process, and are recognized under the World Trade Organization (WTO) through its Agreement on the Application of Sanitary and Phytosanitary Measures (SPS Agreement).

The process of developing a new or revised ISPM is managed by the Standards Committee of the IPPC. The Standards Committee is composed of technical experts representing all the regions of FAO. ISPMs are based upon scientific principles, existing trade policies and technical information. Drafts are initially developed by selected technical experts who are members of panels or working groups. The Technical Panel on Forest Quarantine (TPFQ) addresses forestry-related quarantine issues. The TPFQ may require specific technical information for its standard setting work. TPFQ has relied on the International Forestry Quarantine Research Group (IFQRG), an independent body of research scientists

---

[10] The titles of all existing ISPMs and a short summary are given in Annex 3.

and representatives of national regulatory agencies and the forest sector, to provide this material. The Standards Committee reviews draft standards prepared by the expert drafting groups and finalizes them for "country consultation", a process of international consultation on the standard. Contracting parties of the IPPC may comment and suggest revisions of the draft standard, often after national consultation with affected industries, other government departments, non-governmental organizations, etc. The revisions are negotiated until a draft is developed that is unanimously approved by all contracting parties at an annual meeting of the CPM. The process of developing a new ISPM can take several years.

Contracting parties to the IPPC are required to:
- set up a national plant protection organization (NPPO);[11]
- designate an official IPPC contact point;
- prescribe and adopt phytosanitary measures;
- certify exports;
- regulate imports;
- cooperate internationally;
- share information on pests[12] and regulations;
- cooperate in the development of ISPMs.

NPPOs are the government agencies within the IPPC member countries that implement the phytosanitary standards by developing and enforcing national regulations. They undertake pest risk analyses for the establishment of phytosanitary measures; manage pest surveillance; report to other countries on pest status; coordinate the control of pests; and establish and monitor pest free areas. When required they also issue phytosanitary certificates confirming that consignments have met an importing country's requirements. They also take responsibility for ensuring phytosanitary security of consignments from certification until export; conduct verification inspections and, if necessary, require treatment of consignments or where appropriate, destruction or refusal of entry.

Because pests do not recognize international borders, NPPOs frequently have to work with neighbouring countries to prevent pest entry, establishment and spread. This collaboration may be done through regional plant protection organizations (RPPOs). RPPOs assist in coordinating regulations to deal with regional phytosanitary issues raised by NPPOs. RPPOs gather and disseminate information and may identify priorities for regional standards which may become the basis for new ISPMs. Usually it is an NPPO, or sometimes an RPPO, which requests that the IPPC develop a new ISPM, or revise an existing one, to deal with a particular phytosanitary issue.

---

[11] The full list of NPPOs and RPPOs and their contact persons can be found on the IPPC Web site: www.ippc.int.

[12] Any species, strain or biotype of plant, animal or pathogenic agent injurious to plants or plant products (ISPM No. 05, 2010).

4.2 PEST RISK ANALYSIS

Pest risk involves a wide range of organisms that can potentially be associated with forest commodities such as bacteria, fungi, insects, mites, molluscs, nematodes, viruses and parasitic plants. The pest risk associated with the trade in forest commodities is evaluated by individual countries. Countries must ensure that their phytosanitary import requirements are based on science, are proportional to

Framework for pest risk analysis (ISPM No. 02 [2007]); Guidelines for the export, shipment, import and release of biological control agents and other beneficial organisms (ISPM No. 03 [2005]); Pest risk analysis for quarantine pests including analysis of environmental risks and living modified organisms (ISPM No. 11 [2004]); Pest risk analysis for regulated non-quarantine pests (ISPM No. 21 [2004])

the pest risks, and have minimal impacts on trade.

Pest risk analysis (PRA) can be carried out for a particular pest, for a commodity (which considers all the potential pests it might carry) from a particular country or region of origin, or even more broadly for a pathway. The evaluation of pest risk for a proposed import commodity has several steps. First, a clear description of the commodity and its level of processing (what processes have been applied) is needed. Then a draft list of pests potentially associated with that commodity is prepared from scientific literature and historical records of pests that have been detected on the commodity in other countries.

Next, each potential pest is assessed as to:
- whether it is present in the exporting country and importing country;
- whether it is associated with the commodity or other pathway;
- whether the pest can enter, find suitable habitats, establish and spread in the importing country;
- whether, and to what extent, it will cause economic damage in the importing country.

This assessment requires an understanding of the ecology and behaviour of each organism, including the range of suitable hosts, its life stages, method and rate of reproduction, length of its life cycle and climatic requirements. Furthermore, the potential impacts of the pest on industry, the environment and international trade are evaluated.

The result of this process is an assessment of the pest risk for each organism. When the risks of pests associated with a particular commodity, group of commodities, or the pest(s) associated with a conveyance are considered, this is referred to as a pathway risk analysis.

This assessment of pest risk is one of the inputs to the completed PRA. The pest risk will determine the need for phytosanitary measures. The PRA also includes consideration of various phytosanitary measures to manage the pest risk.

Lack of information is often a major constraint in assessing the pest risk of forest commodities. There may be insufficient information about the organisms associated with a commodity, including their entry, establishment and spread, or on effective treatments or measures to reduce risk. Other information gathering problems may arise from: language of publications; limited or no access to databases; and an inability to predict the economic or environmental impacts. Insufficient or inadequate information results in high uncertainty of pest risk assessment and may lead to a more unjustifiably restrictive import requirement.

4.3 REGULATION OF WOOD PACKAGING MATERIAL

Regulation of wood packaging material in international trade (ISPM No. 15 [2009])

Wood packaging material (WPM) is often used to support, protect or carry goods during transport. WPM includes pallets, boxes or dunnage used in a container, aircraft or ship's hold to secure a variety of trade goods. WPM is sometimes made from low quality wood. Untreated WPM can provide a pathway for a number of significant forest pests, such as *Anoplophora glabripennis* (Asian longhorned beetle) and *Bursaphelenchus xylophilus* (pinewood nematode). The pests may occur at the surface of the wood (e.g. bark beetles, moths and other insects, fungi) or deep inside the wood (e.g. boring beetles, nematodes, fungi).

In recognition of this high risk pathway, ISPM No. 15 was developed. This standard requires that wood packaging materials are treated to kill pests existing in or on the wood, before being moved in international trade. The standard recognizes two treatments: heat treatment, in which the wood is heated to a minimum of 56 °C throughout the profile of the wood for a minimum of 30 minutes; and methyl bromide fumigation at specific concentrations, timings and procedures.

The standard requires that wood be debarked. Where fumigation is used, the debarking process must occur before fumigation. Long thin pieces of bark are allowed to remain after the debarking process if these pieces are no wider than 3 cm (regardless of the length). If bark pieces are wider than 3 cm, they must be short enough so that the wood will dry out before bark beetles can develop. Therefore wide pieces of bark cannot have surface area greater than 50 cm^2.

For many countries methyl bromide is the only available treatment to manage pest risks of WPM, and as such it is recognized in ISPM No. 15. The IPPC recognizes that methyl bromide is an ozone-depleting substance and its use should be limited as much as possible. Many countries have, under the Montreal Protocol,[13] already banned its use and others have announced their intention to do so. The urgency of finding alternatives to methyl bromide continues to remain a key priority in the work programme of the IPPC. Private companies and governments are working to identify additional treatments for use in rendering wood packaging material free of pests.

The standard also states that treated wood must be marked according to the ISPM No. 15 requirements. The mark consists of a box containing:
- an IPPC symbol;
- a country code;

---

[13] The Montreal Protocol on Substances that Deplete the Ozone Layer, as adjusted and/or amended in London 1999, Copenhagen 1992, Vienna 1995, Montreal 1997, Beijing 1999.

- a producer/treatment provider code;
- a treatment code (HT for heat treatment or MB for methyl bromide).

The mark must appear on two opposite sides of the wood packaging unit. WPM that meets all these requirements is said to be "compliant". For more details about the mark, see ISPM No. 15.

The application of treatments and use of the specific identification mark are carried out under the authority of the NPPO in the country of manufacture, to ensure that the treatment providers are actually treating the wood to meet ISPM No. 15 standards. The mark provides the basis for securing entry into countries.

For the working life of the wood packaging unit, it need only be treated once, as long as it remains intact. However, when a unit of wood packaging is repaired (meaning less than one-third of the unit is replaced), the repaired portion of the unit should be made with treated wood and each added component must be individually marked in accordance with ISPM No. 15. Alternatively the entire unit can be retreated and remarked. When a unit is remanufactured (more than one-third of the unit is replaced) the entire unit must be re-treated, old marks removed and a new mark applied.

Note that not all wooden articles that carry trade goods need regulation. Wood packaging made from manufactured wood – such as plywood, fibreboard or oriented strand board – is not regulated as the processes used in the production of these wood products (heat, pressure and glue) assure that they are pest free. Similarly, barrels where sufficient heat is used in processing the staves (i.e. whisky barrels) and wood packaging materials that are made entirely of components less than 6 mm thick are not regulated under ISPM No. 15.

The wood packaging materials standard is a good example of how forest industries and NPPOs have successfully worked together to develop and implement phytosanitary measures.

An example of the IPPC mark on wood packaging material including: the ISPM No. 15 symbol, an ISO two letter country code (ID for Indonesia) followed by a unique number assigned by the NPPO to the producer, and the ISPM No. 15 treatment code (HT for heat treatment)

4.4 PEST MANAGEMENT

Guidelines for pest eradication programmes
(ISPM No. 09 [1998])

The NPPO or other appropriate regulatory authority should be informed when a new pest has been introduced to an area. The NPPO may arrange for official diagnostic confirmation in order to decide whether a pest management programme is needed. Where local diagnostic expertise is limited, the NPPO may contact other NPPOs to whom specimens can be sent for official identification. Such collaboration can save time. The NPPO is obliged to report new pests to the IPPC (see Section 4.7).

Once establishment of a new pest has been confirmed, the possibility of eradication or containment of the pest should be evaluated. If the pest is new and considered to pose a serious risk, the response must be immediate and effective if eradication is to be successful. The NPPO may wish to regulate the pest and initiate an official control programme to prevent further introductions. Even if the pest is too widespread to be eradicated, preventing further introductions will help keep the genetic diversity of the pest low and/or stop more virulent strains from entering the country.

Having a contingency plan in advance of finding a pest, previously approved by all stakeholders, will help save time in the planning stages. The plan should deal with matters such as what needs to be done, how it will be implemented, who will be responsible and who will pay. In many cases, coordination is needed between the NPPO, other government departments, local government authorities, industry sectors and commercial bodies to implement the plan. The knowledge and expertise of forestry experts is essential for successful application of appropriate management measures. Contingency plans should be reviewed frequently to reflect new data or to take into account new experiences in dealing with a particular pest or one with similar characteristics, both locally and in other countries.

If there is no pest-specific plan available, then referring to a generic all-purpose plan may still be useful. Obviously some elements of a pest-specific plan cannot be included in a generic plan, however, such a general contingency plan may provide an immediate framework for developing an effective action plan quickly if a new or unforeseen pest is detected.

The essential elements of a contingency plan include:
- understanding the biology and possible impacts of the pest;
- defining the objectives of the plan;
- establishing response actions that should be implemented (e.g. surveillance, sampling, registration of pesticides, safeguarding potentially infested sites, regulatory actions and destruction of infested articles);
- identifying who is responsible;
- testing the plan by conducting a trial run;
- identifying the resource limitations of involved agencies;
- developing a communication plan (for stakeholders, partners, other NPPOs, the public and media);

- determining when to end an eradication programme (either due to success or failure).

To make sure eradication measures have the best chance of success, four important questions must be answered.

- What is the current and potential pest distribution?
- What are the pathways for entry in to the area?
- How does the pest spread?
- How can the pest be controlled?

To determine the pest distribution and thus the area within which containment and eradication measures are to be taken, delimiting surveys, i.e. surveys to determine the extent of spread of an introduction, must be conducted (see Section 4.6). It may not be possible to carry out an effective survey until signs or symptoms are most likely to be evident, depending on pest biology.

Good record-keeping of actions undertaken during eradication efforts is essential and will help when considering which elements worked best, which did not (and why not), and therefore what might be done differently in the event of a recurrence in the future.

A way of determining the success of eradication needs to be developed on a case by case basis. For example, eradication might be declared a success if surveys fail to detect signs of the pest at any stage of its existence over a specified period of time. It is suggested that this period should be at least twice as long as the life cycle of the pest.

The efficacy of the measures will need to be monitored on a continuous basis and stakeholders will need to be kept informed, especially if changes in strategy are under consideration. It is also important to share best control practices and related information at the global level; this will assist other NPPOs dealing with similar pests and situations. The criteria for determining when changes are appropriate will also need to be agreed on and communicated in advance to stakeholders, trading partners and neighbouring NPPOs. Ideally, stakeholders should be part of the review process as they may have a better understanding of the impacts of proposed changes on their operations than the NPPO, and may be able to suggest alternative approaches.

Sometimes it may not be possible to eradicate the pest. In this case, a procedure should be developed to help decide when to stop trying to eradicate the pest. It may be necessary to change the strategy to a policy of containment and management of the risk. An example of the evolution of a response strategy is given in Box 13.

The appearance of a new pest, and the measures taken to control it, will inevitably have an impact on a wide range of stakeholders. It is important to ensure that key stakeholders understand the potential impact the pest might have, both in general and on their businesses. It is therefore recommended that key stakeholders are identified and given the opportunity to comment on the pest management options.

It is also important for stakeholders and others to understand the economic and other impacts of eradication measures, including the costs and benefits of all potential actions. Impacts may include for example, destruction of plants, loss of biodiversity, lost business revenues, loss of export markets, or the cost of applying pre-export treatment to regulated commodities. An economic impact assessment will often help to determine when the cost of action becomes more expensive than the losses incurred. If the risks of both the pest and the pest eradication programme are fully understood, then stakeholder support for the measures taken is more likely.

BOX 13

Emergency response and exit strategy for the introduction of *Dendroctonus micans* in the United Kingdom

Dendroctonus micans (great spruce bark beetle) is regarded as a major pest of spruce (*Picea* spp.) from eastern Siberia to the west of Europe. It lives and breeds under the bark, destroying the cambium which weakens and, in extreme cases, kills the tree. This beetle was first discovered in the United Kingdom in 1982. Following confirmation of the introduction of the insect, an outbreak management team was established consisting of NPPO and industry personnel to develop a strategy for pest eradication. The strategy initially focused on surveillance, control of wood movement, and sanitation felling of potentially infested trees.

Initial surveillance showed that only parts of the United Kingdom were infested. The area was brought under regulation so that movement of wood out of the area was only permitted if the wood was bark-free or originated from specifically identified pest free areas. All trees found to be infested were felled, peeled of bark to remove obvious infestation and the wood taken to an approved sawmill for processing. For all logs with bark, movement was only permitted within the regulated area to an approved sawmill. To be approved, a sawmill had to install effective debarking equipment and have facilities available for managing bark debris.

Communication tools regarding the risks and established phytosanitary measures were developed. These included publicity leaflets and vehicle windshield stickers.

An inspector was designated to provide advice and guidance to the industry, to oversee surveillance and to monitor compliance at sawmills and other places. Penalties were imposed on offenders.

In the late 1980s, a fourth element was added to the management strategy. A biological control agent, the predator *Rhizophagus grandis*, was introduced and released. The containment programme was maintained to slow the spread of the beetle until populations of the predator could become widely established.

In 2005 eradication efforts were abandoned. *D. micans* was so widespread that it no longer qualified as a quarantine pest. Any new outbreaks elsewhere in the country are now routinely treated by the release of the predator and nature is allowed to take its course. The emergency response slowed the spread of the pest while scientists developed this long-term solution. Today, tree mortality has been reduced to less than one percent of infested trees, compared with 10 percent or more prior to the introduction of the biological control agent.

Dendroctonus micans *(great spruce bark beetle) and the predator* Rhizophagus grandis

4.5 SYSTEMS APPROACHES

A systems approach uses at least two independent phytosanitary measures that cumulatively reduce the pest risk in order for the commodity to meet the requirements of the importing country.

> *The use of integrated measures in a systems approach for pest risk management* (ISPM No. 14 [2002])

Systems approaches provide the opportunity to consider many procedures that can help reduce risk from pre-planting to final use. Systems approaches can provide equivalent alternatives to a single more expensive or limiting measure such as pesticide treatments or prohibition of movement. For example, removing all bark from roundwood by squaring the log, combined with sawing the wood into specific dimensions and visual inspection of the wood during processing, may provide the same level of phytosanitary protection as fumigation of the wood. Refer to ISPM No. 24 for more information about equivalency of phytosanitary measures. Systems approaches can be even better than a single measure if that single measure is uncertain or unreliable. A systems approach should be technically justified. An example of a systems approach is provided in Box 14.

A systems approach in forestry manages the risk of pests in wood and wood products by using a combination of independent measures, from selection of genetic material and site preparation activities to post-harvest treatment and handling to transportation and distribution. Many of the practices suggested in Chapter 3 could be used in a systems approach (see Box 10 in Section 3.8). A systems approach

> **BOX 14**
> **Application of a systems approach for the export of untreated logs**
>
> Trading untreated logs internationally is often considered a significant pest risk. While trading more processed logs is the preferred option, in this particular example, two countries developed a bilateral agreement to allow trade in untreated logs under very closely controlled conditions. The importers wanted logs with bark because bark is used as fuel for running the processing mill. Leaving the bark on logs also prevents drying and splitting of wood during transport. Also, fumigation treatments could be done more efficiently in the importing country. Therefore, a bilateral agreement was developed to allow trade.
>
> The bilateral agreement used more than two different independent risk management measures in a systems approach to cumulatively reduce the pest risk. The consignments must be:
> - free of visible pests prior to transport by inspection;
> - transported only during a specific low risk window of time;
> - unloaded and stored in a special zone that does not have suitable hosts for pests that might come in on the imported logs;
> - fumigated within a few days of entry and then processed.

may integrate silvicultural practices such as pruning, thinning and tree salvage as well as field treatment, post-harvest disinfestation, inspection and culling. It might also include risk management measures designed to prevent contamination or re-infestation, such as maintaining the integrity of lots, requiring pest-proof packaging, or screening areas where the commodity is assembled or stored. Likewise, procedures such as pest surveillance, trapping and sampling can also be incorporated.

A systems approach can also include measures that do not kill pests or reduce their presence but do reduce their potential for entry or establishment. Such measures may include designated harvest or shipping periods, restrictions on certain conditions of the commodity (such as requiring that logs be debarked or fumigated or both), the use of resistant hosts, and limited distribution or restricted use at the destination.

Systems approaches range in complexity and rigour. The simplest type could be simply a combination of at least two independent measures. A more complex systems approach would involve a careful analysis of the most effective opportunities to reduce pest risk, followed by selection of critical control points that are monitored to ensure that pest populations remain within acceptable tolerances.

4.6 SURVEILLANCE

Guidelines for surveillance (ISPM No. 06 [1997])

The terms "surveillance" and "survey" are often confused. Survey is only one component of surveillance. According to ISPM No. 06, surveillance is an official process which collects and records data on pest occurrence or absence by survey, monitoring and other procedures such as literature reviews.

A country may engage in pest surveillance to:
• detect new pests for rapid eradication or containment;
• facilitate trade by providing information about pests and their distribution within the country's territory;
• justify the use of regulations to prevent the entry of a pest that does not occur in the importing country.

Surveillance and survey activities may be required in many locations, especially: storage places where commodities are assembled for export; points of entry and nearby forested areas; and facilities that receive large quantities of imported goods.

There are two major kinds of surveillance: general surveillance and specific surveys. General surveillance is more passive and gathers information on the distribution of pests of concern. Specific surveys are more active and obtain information on pests at a specific site within an area (e.g. a harvest location, the area around exporting sawmills, ports and airports) over a defined period of time. Certain plants and plant products, such as furniture may be included as well.

The NPPO is responsible for gathering and maintaining information for general surveillance. A variety of sources may be used, including FAO, forestry agencies, research institutions, universities, scientific societies (including amateur specialists), land managers, consultants, museums, the general public, scientific and trade journals, pest databases and unpublished material.

To keep these data sources up-to-date, the forestry community can help by monitoring pest situations and reporting to the NPPO or other pest professionals when unusual pests or changes in pest distribution are detected. Monitoring for new pests can also be undertaken by botanical gardens, arboreta and other locations that routinely plant exotic plant materials. A well-organized diagnostic and reporting system is needed to support this effort.

FORESTRY COMMISSION, GREAT BRITAIN

Forester conducting a survey and recording survey data for red band needle blight (Mycosphaerella pini) *in the United Kingdom*

Specific surveys are carried out to detect a particular pest, to identify the extent of the distribution of a pest, to monitor for the presence of a pest in an area or site, or to document the absence of specific pests in order to support the designation of pest free areas (see Section 4.8). These are official surveys that follow a plan that is approved by the NPPO.

Methods for monitoring introduced pests will vary according to the species being monitored and the conditions under which they are monitored. Surveillance and survey activities for introduced pests should emphasize early detection, before major damage occurs and before the pest species has spread over a large area. Effective monitoring tools may include inspections of commodities and packing materials at points of entry, pheromone traps, visual surveys, aerial surveys, planting and monitoring of sentinel or indicator species, and monitoring of artificially stressed trees.

Locations receiving large amounts of imported goods have often proved to be the centre of an infestation, when the establishment of new pests are investigated. Therefore, a survey for pests which are only likely to be present as a result of a recent introduction might focus on possible entry points and pathways of spread (e.g. a specific type of imported nursery plant, a type of sawnwood, or a handicraft such as a wooden birdhouse or carving) and sites where imported commodities are stored, marketed or used as planting material. The survey methodology used must be scientifically based. The selection of survey procedures may be determined by the type of sign or symptom by which the pest can be recognized. Surveys are normally designed to maximize the probability of finding pests.

Personnel involved in surveillance activities should receive periodic training with updates in the identification of pests of concern, especially after agreements are developed with new trading partners or for new forest commodities. These responsible persons should be well-equipped and trained in sampling methods, preservation and transportation of samples for identification, and record keeping. Diagnostic expertise is necessary for verifying the identity of pests. International experts are often available to assist with diagnosis. Samples of identified pest specimens must be kept in safe storage conditions. These are called "voucher specimens or cultures" and are useful in resolving disputes and for confirming identification of further specimens; these should be kept in "reference collections". Maintaining a specimen is also necessary because taxonomic revision can lead to changes in a species definition, i.e. where one species is recognized as a complex of species. When this happens, reference specimens should be re-evaluated to keep records up to date.

For both general surveillance and specific surveys, data quality is important. The records kept should be appropriate for the intended purpose, for example to support specific pest risk analyses, the establishment of pest free areas, or the preparation of pest lists.

Reporting new pests should be encouraged through public education and awareness programmes. Public availability of data and information on the distribution, biology and description of pests may facilitate the reporting of new pest finds. This information should be shared as early as possible, even for pests that have not yet arrived in a country but which have the potential to enter and establish. A clear structure for reporting new pests should be established.

4.7 PEST REPORTING

Signatories to the IPPC have an obligation to report pests when they are identified as a potential threat to trading partners or neighbouring countries, e.g. a new occurrence or a change in pest

Pest reporting (ISPM No. 17 [2002]); *Determination of pest status in an area* (ISPM No. 8 [1998])

status. Official pest reports need to be made by the IPPC contact point (usually the NPPO). The governing body of the IPPC (the CPM) has agreed that pest reporting obligations may be met online at www.ippc.int.

Pest reports are necessary:
- when a new pest is found or there is a sudden increase or decrease in an established or new pest population;
- when the success or failure of eradication of pests is verified;
- in the case of any unexpected situation associated with an established pest, or change in geographical distribution, that increases the pest risk to the reporting country, neighbouring countries or trading partners (e.g. a rapid increase in pest populations, a change in host range or the development of a new, more vigorous strain or biotype).

The detection of a new pathway or the absence of a pest as a result of a specific survey should also be reported.

The rapid expansion of the global economy and the small number of taxonomic experts make it difficult to maintain accurate pest lists for all forest commodities. Better international collaboration is needed to overcome this obstacle. The RPPOs of North America and Europe maintain Web-based reporting systems (Box 15) for regional updates, but these RPPO reports are not considered official IPPC pest reports unless the country has requested the Secretariat to accept them as such and they are posted on the IPPC Web site.

Pest reporting allows countries to adjust their phytosanitary requirements, based on PRAs, and to take measures as necessary to respond to any changes in risk. It provides

---

BOX 15

Examples of pest reporting in Europe and North America

Two regional plant protection organizations publish their pest reports on the Internet. Anyone may sign up to receive pest alerts regularly by e-mail at these Web sites.
- North American Plant Protection Organization (NAPPO): www.pestalert.org
- European and Mediterranean Plant Protection Organization (EPPO): www.eppo. org/QUARANTINE/Alert_List/alert_list.htm

useful current and historical information for the operation of phytosanitary systems. Accurate information on pest status is essential; it provides the technical justification for phytosanitary measures and helps to minimize unjustified interference with trade.

Pest information that might affect planting and marketing choices can also benefit foresters and assist them in working with NPPOs in planning management measures.

4.8 ESTABLISHMENT AND RECOGNITION OF PEST FREE AREAS AND AREAS OF LOW PEST PREVALENCE

Requirements for the establishment of Pest Free Areas (ISPM No. 04 [1995]);
Requirements for the establishment of pest free places of production and pest free production sites (ISPM No. 10 [1999]);
Recognition of pest free areas and areas of low pest prevalence (ISPM No. 29 [2007])

Exporting countries may be able to establish official pest free areas or areas of low pest prevalence. They may then be able to negotiate agreements with importing countries to allow export of regulated commodities from those areas, which may help them gain, maintain or improve market access.

A pest free area (PFA) is defined simply as an area in which a specific pest does not occur. PFAs allow for the export of plants, plant products and other regulated articles without the need for the application of other phytosanitary measures. The official establishment of a PFA must be based on specific survey data. The PFA status must be periodically reviewed by intensive surveys or inspections during the growing season. Documentation should be made available for other regulatory authorities when requested. An example of the use of PFAs is given in Box 16.

A pest free place of production (PFPP) is a place of production where a specific pest does not occur, as determined by the NPPO, even though the pest may be present in the area. The absence of the pest must be demonstrated by scientific evidence such as periodic specific surveys. Trading partners will expect, as a minimum, to see documentation supporting the PFPP declaration.

PFAs and PFPPs are easier to establish in planted forests and more difficult to define in naturally regenerated forests. Naturally regenerated forests have a wider distribution and larger variety of plants and potential pests than planted

---

BOX 16
The movement of regulated commodities between pest free areas

Lymantria dispar (gypsy moth) is a serious pest of deciduous trees in eastern North America. It lays eggs on many commodities and conveyances. It is not present in western North America or Mexico, nor does it occur in portions of provinces or states in eastern Canada and the United States. NPPOs in North America conduct specific annual surveys to identify the exact distribution of the pest, using a very effective pheromone insect trap. The resulting pest information is used to define pest free areas (PFAs) in eastern North America that permit exporters to move regulated articles to non-infested areas.

forests. Therefore, identifying a specific PFA in a naturally regenerated forest would involve surveillance activities that are often too expensive to be practical. In planted forests, the challenge of undertaking surveillance is much more manageable where the hosts are planted in blocks contained within a non-host environment.

4.9 INSPECTION

NPPOs or personnel authorized by the NPPO perform inspections prior to export and at import.

Guidelines for inspection (ISPM No. 23 [2005]); Methodologies for sampling of consignments (ISPM No. 31 [2008])

An export inspection is performed by the exporting country to ensure that a consignment meets the specified phytosanitary requirements of the importing country at the time of inspection. If requirements are met, the inspection may result in the issuance of a phytosanitary certificate by the exporting country's NPPO for the consignment in question.

Import inspection is used to decide whether to accept, detain or reject the imported commodity. Inspection is usually based on visual examination of a commodity. It verifies the identity and integrity of the commodity. It also verifies the effectiveness of phytosanitary measures that have been applied, such as treatments or systems approaches. Visual inspection of wood with the naked eye is very difficult as many pests may be impossible to see, e.g. nematodes. Bundles of wood are obviously difficult to examine. The collection of samples and laboratory analysis can also help to detect pests.

It is extremely useful to keep good records of import pest interceptions. These can help a country decide which commodities need more careful inspection in the future, and which commodities are at lower risk. Good records can also show which countries of origin repeatedly send commodities containing pests, and these records are often the basis for negotiations between countries to help make trade safer. To

Inspecting imported wood in Australia

be really useful, it is important also to have a record of the volume of commodities inspected, so that changes in infestation rate over time can be determined.

In cases of repeated non-compliance (see Section 4.11), the intensity and frequency of import inspections for certain consignments may be increased, or import of the commodity may be stopped. The NPPO of the importing country should also contact the NPPO of the exporting country so that it can identify the source of problems and suggest improvements.

4.10 PHYTOSANITARY CERTIFICATION

Export certification system (ISPM No. 07 [1997]); Guidelines for phytosanitary certificates (ISPM No. 12 [2001]); Consignments in transit (ISPM No. 25 [2006]); Categorization of commodities according to their pest risk (ISPM No. 32 [2009])

NPPOs of exporting countries issue phytosanitary certificates to certify that consignments of plants, plant products or other regulated articles meet the specified phytosanitary import requirements of trading partners, such as demonstrating that a treatment has been performed. The IPPC prescribes a model for this certificate in ISPM No. 12. Phytosanitary certificates should not be required by importing countries for wood products that have been processed so that they have no potential for introducing regulated pests. ISPM No. 32 provides guidance on which commodities need or don't need phytosanitary certification. See also Sections 2.2 and 2.3 of this guide for more information on import and export processes.

The basic elements of the phytosanitary certification process include:
- determining the relevant phytosanitary import requirements of the importing country;
- verifying that the consignment conforms to those requirements at the time of certification;
- issuing a phytosanitary certificate that accurately describes the consignment by species and quantity.

The importing country's NPPO should make available official and current information concerning its requirements. The current requirements for the country of destination may also be obtained by the exporter, and supplied to the exporting country's NPPO.

Individuals or organizations authorized by the NPPO may perform some functions, such as commodity inspections or verification of treatment, prior to the NPPO issuing the phytosanitary certificate.

Importing countries frequently specify requirements for phytosanitary certificates, such as: the use of a specific language; completion by typing or handwritten in legible, capital letters; and the use of specified units. There may be a limited period of validity following inspection or treatment before dispatch of the consignment from the country of origin. A phytosanitary certificate may be rejected or additional information may be requested by the importing country if the phytosanitary certificate:

- is illegible, incomplete or is a non-certified copy;
- includes unauthorized alterations or erasures, conflicting or inconsistent information, or wording that is inconsistent with the instructions or model certificates;
- fails to comply with the specified period of validity;
- certifies prohibited products;
- describes the consignment in a way that does not correspond with the material imported.

Fraudulent certificates should never be accepted and the perpetrator should be subject to legal action.

In some cases, international trade may involve the movement of consignments of regulated articles which pass through a country without being formally imported. This kind of consignment is said to be "in transit". Such movements may present a pest risk to the country of transit, especially if consignments are carried in open containers. Countries may apply technically justified phytosanitary measures to consignments in transit through their territories.

4.11 NON-COMPLIANCE NOTIFICATION

When consignments do not meet phytosanitary import requirements they are considered to be non-compliant. The NPPO of the importing country notifies

Guidelines for the notification of non-compliance and emergency action (ISPM No. 13 [2001])

the NPPO of the exporting country about the non-compliance. The exporting country's NPPO should then follow up with the exporter to ensure that consignments are not rejected in the future.

Non-compliance notifications are provided when there is:
- failure to comply with phytosanitary import requirements;
- detection of regulated pests;
- failure to comply with documentary requirements (e.g. phytosanitary certificates);
- prohibited consignments or prohibited articles in consignments such as soil;
- evidence of failure of specified treatments;
- repeated instances of prohibited articles in small, non-commercial quantities carried by passengers or sent by mail.

4.12 PHYTOSANITARY IMPORT REGULATORY SYSTEMS

An import regulatory system should consist of two components:
- a framework of phytosanitary legislation, regulations and procedures;

Guidelines for a phytosanitary import regulatory system (ISPM No. 20 [2004])

- an official service, the NPPO, responsible for operation or oversight of the system.

NPPOs have the sovereign right to regulate imports to achieve an acceptable level of protection, taking into account their international obligations, in particular the IPPC (1997) and the World Trade Organization (WTO) Agreement on the Application of Sanitary and Phytosanitary Measures (SPS Agreement). When a contracting party implements phytosanitary procedures and regulations, it should try to use measures that reduce risk to an acceptable level with the least negative impacts on trade.

Forest plants (including seeds), wood, wood packaging materials (including dunnage), and used forestry equipment are examples of forestry articles that are regulated in many countries.

5. The way forward

Forest pests are a global problem and consequently it is necessary to look beyond national borders to develop effective solutions. Despite many improvements in phytosanitary protection, introductions of new forest pests continue because of the increase in volume of international trade and speed of transport. Climate change also appears to be increasing the probability of new pest establishment as well as providing conditions that allow some species to become more serious pests in their native range. Foresters and scientists must increase their efforts to work together with national plant protection organizations (NPPOs) to take the actions necessary to prevent pest introduction and spread.

Fortunately, information sharing between people working in forestry and plant health regulators is already helping prevent, detect and eradicate new pest outbreaks. Continued expansion of this networking, and the use of technologies such as the Internet can assist in addressing the challenge of global pest control.

Good forest management practices, such as those described in this guide, can help reduce pest outbreaks and prevent pests from moving around the globe via forest commodities. Integrated pest management begins with planning what to grow and where to grow it. Careful surveillance, the management of forest stands throughout the growing cycle, and good practices during harvest and transport operations can bring quality, low pest-risk products to the international marketplace. Understanding and meeting the phytosanitary requirements of importing countries is necessary and helps enhance the safe movement of forest commodities and reduce overall costs with minimal impacts on international trade.

A number of important international standards for phytosanitary measures (ISPMs) provide guidance that is helpful in reducing forest pest movement in international trade. New ISPMs related to the trade of forest commodities continue to be developed in response to international needs. Currently, standards on wood commodities and forest tree seed are being drafted by the International Plant Protection Convention (IPPC) Technical Panel on Forest Quarantine (TPFQ) and participation of foresters, particularly during the country consultation stage, in the development of these standards is essential.

As new ISPMs are developed, people working in forestry can provide valuable input with their special knowledge and expertise that will help build practical guidelines. In this way, by working together, forest sector personnel, including industry, and NPPOs can promote trade opportunities and help prevent the introduction and spread of forest pests.

References

American Lumber Standard Committee (ALSC). 2005. *American Softwood Lumber Standard.* National Institute of Standards and Technology Voluntary Product Standard PS 20-05. Washington DC, USA, United States Department of Commerce, National Institute of Standards and Technology. Available at: www.alsc.org/greenbook%20collection/ps20.pdf

Animal and Plant Health Inspection Service (APHIS). 2009. Importation of wooden handicrafts from China. *U.S. Federal Register*, Vol. 74, No. 67, Thursday, April 9, 2009, Proposed Rules. Available at: edocket.access.gpo.gov/2009/pdf/E9-8102.pdf

APHIS. 2010. Part 319-Foreign Quarantine Notices. Subpart – Logs, lumber, and other unmanufactured wood articles. APHIS 7CFR 319.40. Available at: http://edocket.access.gpo.gov/cfr_2009/janqtr/pdf/7cfr319.40-1.pdf (Accessed on 12 July 2010)

British Columbia (BC) Ministry of Forests and Range. 2008. *Glossary of forestry terms in British Columbia.* Victoria, BC, Canada. Available at: www.for.gov.bc.ca/hfd/library/documents/glossary

Dunster, J. & Dunster, K. 1996. Dictionary of natural resource management. Vancouver, BC, Canada, UBC Press.

Dykstra, D.P. & Heinrich, R. 1996. FAO model code of forest harvesting practice. Rome, FAO. Available at: www.fao.org/docrep/v6530e/v6530e00.htm

Evans, D. 2000. *Terms of the trade.* Eugene, Oregon, USA, Random Lengths Publications Inc. (4th ed.)

FAO. 1994. *Tree breeding glossary. Glossary of terms used in forest tree improvement.* Field Manual No. 6 (RAS/91/004), UNDP/FAO Regional Project on Improved Productivity of Man-made Forests Through Application of Technological Advances in Tree Breeding and Propagation. Los Banos, the Philippines.

FAO. 2001. *Glossary of biotechnology for food and agriculture – A revised and augmented edition of the glossary of biotechnology and genetic engineering.* By A. Zaid, H.G. Hughes, E. Porceddu & F. Nicholas. Available at: www.fao.org/DOCREP/003/X3910E/X3910E00.htm; www.fao.org/biotech/index_glossary.asp

FAO. 2003. *An illustrated guide to the state of health of trees. Recognition and interpretation of symptoms and damage,* by E. Boa. Rome. Available at: www.fao.org/docrep/007/y5041e/y5041e00.htm

FAO. 2004. UBET – Unified Bioenergy Terminology. Rome, FAO. Available at: www.fao.org/docrep/007/j4504E/j4504e00.htm

FAO. 2005. *FAO Yearbook of Forest Products 1999–2003.* FAO, Rome. Available at: ftp://ftp.fao.org/docrep/fao/012/i0750m/i0750m01.pdf

FAO. 2007. *Global Forest Resources Assessment 2010 – Specification of National Reporting Tables for FRA 2010.* FRA Working Paper 135. Rome. Available at: www.fao.org/forestry/14119-1-0.pdf

FAO. 2010a. *Global Forest Resources Assessment 2010. Main report.* FAO Forestry Paper No. 163. Rome.

FAO. 2010b. Forestry trade flows – FAOSTAT. Available at: http://faostat.fao.org (Accessed October 2010)

FAO. 2010c. AGROVOC – Multilingual Agricultural Thesaurus. Available at: www.fao.org/agrovoc (Accessed 12 July 2010)

FAO/IUFRO. 2002. *Multilingual glossary – forest genetic resources.* Available at: iufro-archive.boku.ac.at/iufro/silvavoc/glossary/index.html

Gordon, D.R., Onderdonk, D.A., Fox, A.M. & Stocker, R.K. 2008. Consistent accuracy of the Australian weed risk assessment system across varied geographies. *Diversity Distributions*, 14: 234–243.

Hillring, B. & Trossero, M. 2006. International wood-fuel trade – an overview. *Energy for Sustainable Development*, X(1): 33–41.

Hubbard, W., Latt, C. & Long, A. 1998. *Forest terminology for multiple-use management.* SS-FOR-11. Gainesville, FL, USA, University of Florida.

International Union for Conservation of Nature (IUCN). 2000. *Guidelines for the prevention of biodiversity loss caused by alien invasive species.* Approved by the IUCN Council, Feb 2000. Gland, Switzerland. Available at: intranet.iucn.org/webfiles/doc/SSC/SSCwebsite/Policy_statements/IUCN_Guidelines_for_the_Prevention_of_Biodiversity_Loss_caused_by_Alien_Invasive_Species.pdf

Martin, J. 1996. *Forestry terms.* Madison, WI, USA, University of Wisconsin-Extension. Publication No. G3018. Available at: basineducation.uwex.edu/woodland/OWW/Pubs/UWEX/G3018.pdf

McNeely, J. A. 1999. The great reshuffling: how alien species help feed the global economy. *In* O.T. Sandlund, P.J. Schei & Viken, Å. eds. *Invasive species and biodiversity management.* Based on a selection of papers presented at the Norway/UN Conference on Alien Species, Trondheim, Norway, pp. 11–31. Population and Community Biology Series, Vol. 24. Dordrecht, the Netherlands, Kluwer Academic Publishers.

McNeill, J., Barrie, F.R., Burdet, H.M., Demoulin, V., Hawksworth, D.L., Marhold, K., Nicolson, D.H., Prado, J., Silva, P.C., Skog, J.E., Wiersema, J.H. & Turland, N.J. 2006. *International Code of Botanical Nomenclature (Vienna Code).* Vienna, International Association for Plant Taxonomy. Available at: ibot.sav.sk/icbn/main.htm

North Carolina State University. 2003. *Understanding forestry terms: A glossary for private landowners.* Woodland Owners Notes. Raleigh, NC, USA, North Carolina Cooperative Extension Service. Available at: www.ces.ncsu.edu/nreos/forest/pdf/WON/won26.pdf

Pheloung, P.C., Williams, P.A. & Halloy, S.R. 1999. A weed risk assessment model for use as a biosecurity tool evaluating plant introductions. *Journal of Environmental Management*, 57, 239–251.

Richardson, D.M. 1998. Forestry trees as invasive aliens. *Conservation Biology*, 12(1): 18–26.

Schuck, A., Päivinen, R., Hytönen, T. & Pajari, B. 2002. *Compilation of forestry terms and definitions.* Internal Report No. 6. Joensuu, Finland, European Forest Institute. Available at: www.efi.int/files/attachments/publications/ir_06.pdf

Tainter, F.H. & Baker, F.A. 1996. *Principles of Forest Pathology.* New York, John Wiley and Sons, Inc.

UNECE, FAO, EUROSTAT and ITTO. 2008. Joint UNECE/FAO/EUROSTAT/ITTO Forest Sector Questionnaire – Definitions. Available at: www.unece.org/timber/mis/jfsq2008

United Nations Environment Programme-World Conservation Monitoring Centre (UNEP-WCMC). 2010. Glossary of Biodiversity Terms. Available at: www.unep-wcmc.org/reception/glossary.htm (accessed 07 July 2010)

van den Bosch, R., Messenger, P.S. & Gutierrez, A.P. 1981. *An introduction to biological control.* New York, Plenum Press.

West Virginia University. 1998. *Glossary of forestry terms.* Rev. 8/98.

World Resources Institute (WRI), International Union for Conservation of Nature (IUCN), United Nations Environment Programme (UNEP). 1992. *Global biodiversity strategy: guidelines for action to save, study, and use earth's biotic wealth sustainably and equitably.* Washington, DC, WRI. Available at: pdf.wri.org/globalbiodiversitystrategy_bw.pdf

van Wilgen, B.W., Richardson, D.M., le Maitre, D.C., Marais, C. & Magadlela, D. 2001. The economic consequences of alien plant invasions: examples of impacts and approaches to sustainable management in South Africa. *Environment, Development and Sustainability*, 3: 145–168.

Annex 1
Examples of forest pest introductions and their impacts

Agrilus planipennis, emerald ash borer

IMPACTS

Has caused death and decline of millions of trees in Canada and the United States; predicted to ultimately kill most ash in forests, urban plantings and shelterbelts. Costs in the United States are expected to exceed US$1 billion per year for the next 10 years. In the Russian Federation, most ash trees within 100 km of Moscow have been killed; infestation is spreading rapidly and European forests are threatened.

PATHWAYS

Movement of plants, wood and wood products in particular fuelwood, and wood packaging materials; flight and wind dispersal

Adult emerald ash borer, Agrilus planipennis

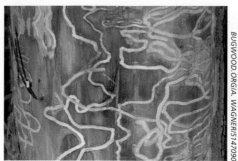

Larval galleries

Exit holes

Infested tree exhibiting root sprouts and crown dieback

MAIN HOSTS

Fraxinus spp. (ash), *Juglans* spp. (walnut), *Pterocarya* spp. (Japanese wingnut), *Ulmus* spp. (elm)

NATIVE RANGE

China, Democratic People's Republic of Korea, Japan, Mongolia, Republic of Korea, far east of the Russian Federation

INTRODUCED RANGE

Europe: Russian Federation (Moscow and surrounding area)
North America: Canada, United States of America

SYMPTOMS AND DAMAGE

Larvae infest upper trunk and lower portions of main branches causing yellowing and thinning of foliage; dieback and death of trees normally within 3 years.

Cinara cupressivora, cypress aphid

IMPACTS
Serious damage to forests in Africa, Europe and South America. Rapidly spread through Africa after accidental introduction into Malawi in 1986. By 1990, trees worth approximately US$44 million were lost plus US$14.6 million per year through reductions in annual growth increment. In Kenya, it was estimated that it might kill up to 50 percent of all cypress trees during the 30-year harvest cycle.

PATHWAYS
Movement of nursery stock; flight and wind dispersal

MAIN HOSTS
Cupressus spp. (cypress), *Juniperus* spp. (juniper)

NATIVE RANGE
Europe and Near East – from eastern Greece to the Islamic Republic of Iran

INTRODUCED RANGE
Africa: Burundi, Democratic Republic of the Congo, Ethiopia, Kenya, Malawi, Mauritius, Morocco, Rwanda, South Africa, Uganda, United Republic of Tanzania, Zambia, Zimbabwe

Cypress aphids, Cinara cupressivora

Insects

BUGWOOD.OFG.I.D. IWARD/2912011

Insects

BUGWOOD.ORG/W.M. CIESLA/3948003

Damage, Kenya

Europe: France, Italy, Spain, United Kingdom
Latin America and the Caribbean: Chile, Colombia
Near East: Jordan, Syrian Arab Republic, Turkey, Yemen

SYMPTOMS AND DAMAGE
Sap sucking on terminal growth of young and old trees retards new growth and causes desiccation of stems. Progressive dieback on heavily infested trees.

Sirex noctilio, European woodwasp

Insects

IMPACTS

Threat to certain forests and the forest sector causing considerable damage and costs for control: New Zealand, tree losses reached 30 percent by the 1940s; Australia (Tasmania), about 40 percent of trees died in late 1950s; Australia, 5 million trees killed during 1987–1989 outbreak. A serious threat to the forest industry in South Africa, causing considerable losses in Eastern Cape and KwaZulu-Natal Provinces. In Brazil, the potential economic impacts are approximately US$25 million annually.

PATHWAYS

Flight and wind dispersal; movement of sawnwood, untreated pine logs and wood packaging materials

MAIN HOSTS

Pinus spp. (pine)

NATIVE RANGE

Asia, Europe, northern Africa (Algeria, Morocco, Tunisia)

BUGWOOD.ORG/D.R. LANCE/1414001

Adult male sirex woodwasp, Sirex noctilio

Insects

BUGWOOD.ORG/P. KLASMER/1349006

BUGWOOD.ORG/P. KLASMER/1349007

Larval tunnelling   *Damage*

INTRODUCED RANGE
Africa: South Africa
Asia and the Pacific: Australia (including Tasmania), New Zealand
Latin America and the Caribbean: Argentina, Brazil, Chile, Uruguay
North America: Canada, United States of America

SYMPTOMS AND DAMAGE
Drills into wood to lay eggs; injects toxic mucus and a fungus (*Amylostereum areolatum*) which may result in wilting and tree death; foliage turns from green to yellow to reddish-brown. Larval tunnelling damages wood; fungus causes white rot.

Leptocybe invasa, blue-gum chalcid

IMPACTS
Major pest of young eucalypt trees and seedlings. Native to Australia, currently spreading through Africa, Asia and the Pacific, Europe, Latin America and the Near East.

PATHWAYS
Movement of nursery stock; international air traffic; flight and wind dispersal

MAIN HOSTS
Eucalyptus spp. (eucalypt)

NATIVE RANGE
Australia

INTRODUCED RANGE
Africa: Algeria, Kenya, Morocco, South Africa, United Republic of Tanzania, Uganda
Asia and the Pacific: Cambodia, India, New Zealand, Thailand, Viet Nam
Europe: France, Greece, Italy, Portugal, Spain
Latin America and the Caribbean: Argentina, Brazil
Near East: Iraq, Islamic Republic of Iran, Israel, Jordan, Lebanon, Syrian Arab Republic, Turkey

Ovipositing female blue-gum chalcid, Leptocybe invasa

Insects

G. ALLARD

Young galls on eucalypt branches and leaf petioles, United Republic of Tanzania

G. ALLARD

Leptocybe *damage: older galls with exit holes on eucalypt branches and leaf petioles, United Republic of Tanzania*

SYMPTOMS AND DAMAGE

Developing larvae form bump-shaped galls on leaf midribs, petioles and stems of new growth of young eucalypt trees, coppice and nursery seedlings. Severely attacked trees show leaf fall, gnarled appearance, loss of growth and vigour, stunted growth, lodging, dieback and eventually tree death.

Cryphonectria parasitica, chestnut blight

IMPACTS

American chestnut (*Castanea dentata*) was one of the most abundant hardwoods in the eastern United States of America and is now nearly extinct because of chestnut blight – which shows how a disease can fundamentally alter an entire ecosystem. Chestnut trees are very important economically, producing durable wood (for furniture, construction) and nuts (cash crop, staple food for wildlife). The impact of chestnut blight on the forest sector in Turkey has contributed to the migration of the young workforce from rural to urban environments.

PATHWAYS

Movement of infected nursery stock, wood or bark; spread locally through poor harvesting techniques and by wind or blown rain

MAIN HOSTS

Castanea spp. (chestnut), *Quercus* spp. (oak)

NATIVE RANGE

Asia

BUGWOOD.ORG/A. KUNCA/1415061

Symptoms of chestnut blight, Cryphonectria parasitica *– canker and bark necrosis*

BUGWOOD.ORG/A. KUNCA/5382673

Symptoms – wilting leaves

INTRODUCED RANGE

Africa: Tunisia

Europe: Austria, Belgium, Bosnia and Herzegovina, Croatia, France, Georgia, Germany, Greece, Hungary, Italy, Poland, Portugal, Russian Federation, Slovakia, Slovenia, Spain, Switzerland, The Former Yugoslav Republic of Macedonia, Turkey, Ukraine

Near East: Islamic Republic of Iran

North America: Canada, United States of America

SYMPTOMS AND DAMAGE

Infects above-ground parts of trees only, creating cankers that expand, girdle and eventually kill tree branches and trunks.

Ophiostoma ulmi and Ophiostoma novo-ulmi, Dutch elm disease

IMPACTS

Dutch scientists first isolated the fungus in the 1920s, hence the name of this vascular wilt disease. One of the most severe diseases in the temperate world where elms are grown. Hundreds of millions of healthy mature elms lost in northern Asia, Europe and North America. Major pandemic across Northern Hemisphere from 1920s to 1940s. First reported in France, then spread through continental Europe and the United States of America, decimating elm populations. Disease declined in Europe but re-emerged when a second, more virulent species established in the United Kingdom, most of Europe, and the United States of America. Insect vectors: *Scolytus* spp. and *Hylurgopinus rufipes* (bark beetles).

PATHWAYS

Movement of infested or infected planting material, fuelwood and logs with bark

MAIN HOSTS

Ulmus spp. (elm)

NATIVE RANGE

Asia

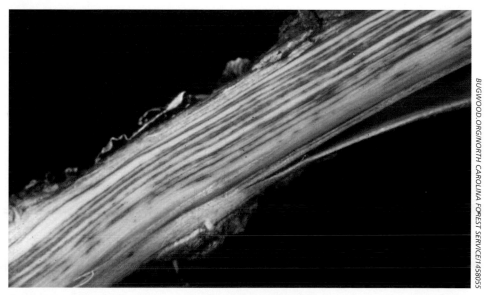

BUGWOOD.ORG/NORTH CAROLINA FOREST SERVICE/1458055

Symptoms of Dutch elm disease – streaking of vascular tissue

Symptoms – wilting leaves

Symptoms on American elm, Ulmus americana

INTRODUCED RANGE
Worldwide (temperate regions). Re-introduction of more virulent species from North America to Europe (mid-1960s)

SYMPTOMS AND DAMAGE
Insect vectors carry fungus while feeding on branches; fungus spreads via tree sap throughout tree; can also spread via root grafts from tree to tree. Wilting, yellowing and browning of leaves; branches may be individually infected; brownish streaks of discolouration in branches and stems; symptoms may progress throughout a tree in a single season or take two or more years.

Phytophthora ramorum, sudden oak death, ramorum blight

Diseases

IMPACTS
Attacks various nursery plants and forest trees where it has spread into forests. In the United States of America (California) millions of oak and tanoak trees have died. In the United Kingdom it has recently been found infecting Japanese larch, resulting in significant mortality. Inoculum remains viable in soil for a period of years after removal of infected trees and shrubs, thereby affecting reforestation decisions.

PATHWAYS
Movement of infected or contaminated plant material, growing media, nursery stock and soil carried on vehicles, machinery, footwear and animals

MAIN HOSTS
Quercus spp. (oak), *Lithocarpus densiflorus* (tanoak), *Larix kaempeferi* (Japanese larch), *Rhododendron* spp. (rhododendron, azalea), *Umbellularia californica* (bay laurel), and many other plant species

NATIVE RANGE
Unknown

BUGWOOD.OF G.J. O'BRIEN/1427061

Bleeding on coast live oak (Quercus agrifolia) *resulting from* Phytophthora ramorum *infection*

Diseases

Symptoms on Q. agrifolia   *Symptoms on* Q. agrifolia

INTRODUCED RANGE
Europe: Belgium, Denmark, Finland, France, Germany, Ireland, Italy, Lithuania, the Netherlands, Norway, Poland, Serbia, Slovenia, Spain, Switzerland, Sweden, United Kingdom
North America: United States of America

SYMPTOMS AND DAMAGE
Symptoms on oak/tanoak: stem bark lesions, bleeding basal cankers, branch cankers, crown dieback followed by death. Symptoms on other hosts: leaf lesions, small branch cankers, stem and branch dieback.

Puccinia psidii, eucalyptus rust

IMPACTS

Attacks many genera in the family Myrtaceae, with specific strains causing landscape-scale devastation on particular hosts. First described on guava, this pathogen causes substantial damage to non-native eucalypt plantations in South America.

PATHWAYS

Movement of infected or contaminated plant material, cut foliage, and any items exposed to spores, which can survive for two to three months.

Symptoms of eucalyptus rust, Puccinia psidii

Diseases

CELSO GARCIA AUER

Diseases

MAIN HOSTS
Eucalyptus spp. (eucalypt)

NATIVE RANGE
South and Central America

INTRODUCED RANGE
Latin America and the Caribbean: Cuba, Dominican Republic, Jamaica, Trinidad and Tobago
North America: United States of America (California, Florida, Hawaii, Puerto Rico)

SYMPTOMS AND DAMAGE
Attacks young tissues of plants and can cause deformation of leaves, heavy defoliation of branches, dieback, stunted growth and sometimes death.

Bursaphelenchus xylophilus, pinewood nematode

Nematodes

IMPACTS

Threat to certain pine forests; has caused extensive tree mortality in some areas where it has been introduced; millions of trees killed annually in Japan. Insect-vectors: *Monochamus* spp. (sawyer or longhorned beetles).

PATHWAYS

Flight of adult vector beetles; movement of infected and vector-infested planting material, fuelwood, timber, wood packaging materials and logs

MAIN HOSTS

Pinus spp. (pine)

NATIVE RANGE

North America

INTRODUCED RANGE

Asia and the Pacific: China, Japan, Republic of Korea
Europe: Portugal

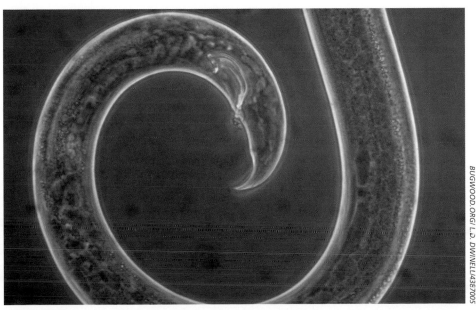

BUGWOOD.ORG/ L.D. DWINELL/4387005

Pinewood nematode, Bursaphelenchus xylophilus

Nematodes

BUGWOOD.ORG/I. TOMMINEN/0725076

Monochamus *sp., the vector of* B. xylophilus

BUGWOOD.ORG/M. OSTRY/1406274

Needle discolouration

BUGWOOD.ORG/M. CIESLA/3948025

Reddish crowns

SYMPTOMS AND DAMAGE

Nematode deposited when adult beetles feed or lay eggs in trees. Presence of nematodes in xylem can result in wilt and mortality; also feed on fungal tissues in dead trees or wood products.

Bursaphelenchus cocophilus, red ring nematode

IMPACTS:

Significant threat to coconut and other palms; young coconut palms succumb easily; palms of various ages affected; no record of palms recovering once infected; disease not recognizable externally; losses up to 80 percent, however, the losses typically range from 10 to 15 percent on coconut and oil palms. Insect vectors: *Rhynchophorus palmarum* and *Dynamis borassi* (palm weevils); *Metamasius hemipterus* (sugarcane weevil), implicated in transmission.

PATHWAYS

Carried by insect vectors that feed on infected palms as larvae and transmit the nematode as adults; movement of infected and vector-infested wood products

Damage caused by the red ring nematode, Bursaphelenchus cocophilus, *including chlorosis and browning of the leaf tips of the oldest leaves of a coconut palm, Brazil*

Nematodes

Nematodes

MAIN HOSTS
Cocos nucifera (coconut), *Elaeis guineensis* and *E. oleifera* (oil palms)

NATIVE RANGE
Latin America and the Caribbean

WORLD DISTRIBUTION
Belize, Brazil, Colombia, Costa Rica, Ecuador, El Salvador, French Guiana, Grenada, Guatemala, Guyana, Honduras, Mexico, Nicaragua, Panama, Peru, Saint Vincent and the Grenadines, Suriname, Trinidad and Tobago, Venezuela

SYMPTOMS AND DAMAGE
Nematode deposited when infected adult beetles feed or lay eggs in the crown of palms. Chlorosis occurs, first at leaf tips of older leaves, which may eventually become brown and dried. Nuts are shed prematurely; crowns of affected coconut palms often topple over (associated also with weevil damage); characteristic internal orange to brick-red coloured ring in trunk cross-section, but can be brownish in colour depending on palm species and variety.

Annex 2
Glossary of terms

These definitions were collected from publications and the Internet. Definitions and terms in forestry and other fields are highly variable, and policy-makers note a lack of common understanding of terms. Many people and organizations have strived to reach some common understandings about definitions. In forestry, FAO and the International Union of Forest Research Organizations (IUFRO) have collaborated for many years in this area (e.g. FAO/IUFRO, 2002). FAO has also developed terms and definitions for the Global Forest Resources Assessment (FRA), taking into consideration recommendations from experts in various fora. It should be noted that the authors of this guide do not intend to confuse readers by listing more than one definition for the same term. Our intention is mainly to alert readers that, even within a particular sector, a different meaning of the same term may exist. Please note that the International Standards for Phytosanitary Measures (ISPMs) use the definitions specified in ISPM No. 05 exclusively. For the latest IPPC definitions, refer to the IPPC Web site (www.ippc.int) as they may be revised.

Area: An officially defined country, part of a country or all or parts of several countries (ISPM No. 05, 2010)

Bark: The layer of a woody trunk, branch or root outside the cambium (ISPM No. 05, 2010)
The tissues of a tree outside the cambium composed of inner living bark and outer dead bark (BC Ministry of Forests and Range, 2008)
The outer part of woody stems and branches. Anatomically it includes all the plant tissues outside the cambium (Evans, 2000)

Biological control: The use of biotic agents such as insects, nematodes, fungi, and viruses for the control of weeds and other forest pests (BC Ministry of Forests and Range, 2008)

Biological control agent: A natural enemy, antagonist or competitor, or other organism, used for pest control (ISPM No. 05, 2010)

Buffer zone: An area surrounding or adjacent to an area officially delimited for phytosanitary purposes in order to minimize the probability of spread of the target pest into or out of the delimited area, and subject to phytosanitary or other control measures, if appropriate (ISPM No. 05, 2010)

A strip of land where disturbances are not allowed, or are closely monitored, to preserve aesthetic and other qualities adjacent to roads, trails, waterways, and recreation sites. (BC Ministry of Forests and Range, 2008)

Certificate: An official document which attests to the phytosanitary status of any consignment affected by phytosanitary regulations (ISPM No. 05, 2010)

Commodity: A type of plant, plant produce, or other article being moved for trade or other purpose (ISPM No. 05, 2010)

Conifer: A tree belonging to the order of Coniferales, usually evergreen, cone bearing and with needles, awl or scalelike leaves such as pine, spruces, firs, tamarack, often called "softwoods" (Martin, 1996)
Any tree that produces seeds in cones, with no fruit structure around the seed. Leaves are usually needles, scales, or narrow and linear in shape, and evergreen (Hubbard *et al.*, 1998)

Consignment: A quantity of plants, plant products and/or other articles being moved from one country to another and covered, when required, by a single phytosanitary certificate (a consignment may be composed of one or more commodities or lots) (ISPM No. 05, 2010)

Contaminating pest: A pest that is carried by a commodity, and in the case of plants and plant products, does not infest those plants or plant products (ISPM No. 05, 2010)

Cut branches: A commodity class for fresh parts of plants intended for decorative use and not for planting (ISPM No. 05, 2010)

Debarked wood: Wood that has been subjected to any process that results in the removal of bark. Debarked wood is not necessarily bark-free wood (ISPM No. 05, 2010)

Delimiting survey: Survey conducted to establish the boundaries of an area considered to be infested by or free from a pest (ISPM No. 05, 2010)

Dunnage: Wood packaging material used to secure or support a commodity but which does not remain associated with the commodity (ISPM No. 05, 2010). An example of dunnage is logs used to wedge heavy objects in a container or ships hold to keep them from moving during shipment.

Ecosystem: A dynamic complex of plant, animal and micro-organism communities and their abiotic environment interacting as a functional unit (ISPM No. 05, 2010)
A functional unit consisting of all the living organisms (plants, animals, and

microbes) in a given area, and all the non-living physical and chemical factors of their environment, linked together through nutrient cycling and energy flow. An ecosystem can be of any size – a log, pond, field, forest, or the earth's biosphere – but it always functions as a whole unit. Ecosystems are commonly described according to the major type of vegetation (i.e. forest, old-growth or range ecosystem) (BC Ministry of Forests and Range, 2008)

Emergency action: A prompt phytosanitary action undertaken in a new or unexpected phytosanitary situation (ISPM No. 05, 2010)

Entry (of a pest): Movement of a pest into an area where it is not yet present, or present but not widely distributed and being officially controlled (ISPM No. 05, 2010)

Eradication: Application of phytosanitary measures to eliminate a pest from an area (ISPM No. 05, 2010)

Establishment: Perpetuation, for the foreseeable future, of a pest within an area after entry (ISPM No. 05, 2010)

Fibreboard: A panel manufactured from fibres of wood or other ligno-cellulosic materials with the primary bond deriving from the felting of the fibres and their inherent adhesive properties (although bonding materials and/or additives may be added in the manufacturing process). It includes fibreboard panels that are flat-pressed and moulded fibreboard products. It is an aggregate comprising hardboard, medium density fibreboard (MDF) and other fibreboard (UNECE *et al.*, 2008)

Field: A plot of land with defined boundaries within a place of production on which a commodity is grown (ISPM No. 05, 2010)

Forest: Land spanning more than 0.5 hectares with trees higher than 5 metres and a canopy cover of more than 10 percent, or trees able to reach these thresholds *in situ*. It does not include land that is predominantly under agricultural or urban land use (FAO, 2007)
A biological community of plants and animals which is dominated by trees and other woody plants (Hubbard *et al.*, 1998)
A plant community with trees and other woody plants dominating (Martin, 1996)
See also Naturally regenerated forest, Planted forest

Forestry: The science of establishing, cultivating, and managing forests and their attendant resources (Hubbard *et al.*, 1998)
The science, art, and practice of managing and using trees, forests, and their associated resources for human benefit (North Carolina State University, 2003)

Fuelwood: Woodfuel where the original composition of the wood is preserved (FAO, 2004)

Fumigation: Treatment with a chemical agent that reaches the commodity wholly or primarily in a gaseous state (ISPM No. 05, 2010)

Genetic diversity: The genetic variability within a population or a species. It is one aspect of biological diversity. Genetic diversity can be assessed at three levels: (a) diversity within breeding populations, (b) diversity between breeding populations; and (c) diversity within the species (FAO/IUFRO, 2002)

Genotype: The genetic constitution of an organism as distinguished from its appearance or phenotype (FAO/IUFRO, 2002)

Habitat: Part of an ecosystem with conditions in which an organism naturally occurs or can establish (ISPM No. 05, 2010)
The environment in which a population or individual lives; includes not only the place where a species is found, but also the particular characteristics of the place (e.g. climate or the availability of suitable food and shelter) that make it especially well suited to meet the life cycle needs of that species (BC Ministry of Forests and Range, 2008)

Handicraft: Commodity class of articles derived or made of natural components of wood, twigs, and vines, and including bamboo poles and garden stakes. Handicrafts include the following products where wood is present: Carvings, baskets, boxes, bird houses, manufactured Christmas trees, garden and lawn/patio furniture (rustic), potpourri, silk trees (typically artificial *Ficus* trees), trellis towers, garden fencing and edging, and other items composed of wood (APHIS, 2009)

Hitch-hiker pest: See Contaminating pest.

Host range: Species capable, under natural conditions, of sustaining a specific pest or other organism (ISPM No. 05, 2010)

Import permit: Official document authorizing importation of a commodity in accordance with specified phytosanitary import requirements (ISPM No. 05, 2010)

Incidence (of a pest): Proportion or number of units in which a pest is present in a sample, consignment, field or other defined population (ISPM No. 05, 2010)
A measurement of the presence and magnitude of pests within a given area (BC Ministry of Forests and Range, 2008)

Indigenous species: Species or genotypes which have evolved in the same area, region or biotope and are adapted to the specific predominant ecological conditions

at the time of establishment. Tree species which have evolved in the same area, region or biotope where the forest stand is growing and are adapted to the specific ecological conditions predominant at the time of the establishment of the stand (Schuck *et al.*, 2002)
Species native to the country or area. Antonym: non-native or exotic (FAO, 1994)
See also Native species

Infestation (of a commodity): Presence in a commodity of a living pest of the plant or plant product concerned. Infestation includes infection (ISPM No. 05, 2010)

Inoculum: Microbial spores or parts (such as mycelium) (FAO, 2001)

Inspection: Official visual examination of plants, plant products or other regulated articles to determine if pests are present and/or to determine compliance with phytosanitary regulations (ISPM No. 05, 2010)

Introduced species: A species occurring in an area outside of its historically known natural range as a result of intentional or accidental dispersal by human activities. Also known as an alien species (WRI, IUCN and UNEP, 1992)
A species, subspecies or lower taxon occurring outside its natural range (past or present) and dispersal potential (i.e. outside the range it occupies naturally or could occupy without direct or indirect introduction or care by humans) (FAO, 2007). This definition refers to trees.
An established species not native to the ecosystem, region or country (FAO/IUFRO, 2002)

Introduction: The entry of a pest resulting in its establishment (ISPM No. 05, 2010)

Invasive species: Species that are non-native to a particular ecosystem and whose introduction and spread cause, or are likely to cause, socio-cultural, economic or environmental harm or harm to human health (FAO, 2007)

Log: Any section of the bole, or of the thicker branches, of a felled tree after limbing and bucking (Dykstra and Heinrich, 1996)
A section of a woody stem bucked to a specific merchantable length for manufacturing into products. Sometimes used more narrowly for a given standard log length, usually of 16 feet, when estimating volume of standing timber (West Virginia University, 1998).
A piece of the woody stem (trunk or limb) of a tree (Martin, 1996)
The bole of a tree; trimmed wood that has not been sawn further than to form cants (APHIS, 2010)

Lot: A number of units of a single commodity, identifiable by its homogeneity of composition, origin etc., forming part of a consignment (ISPM No 5, 2010)

Lumber: Sawn products produced from logs. Also called sawnwood (Dykstra and Heinrich, 1996)

Logs that have been sawn into boards, planks, or structural members such as beams (APHIS, 2010)

A manufactured product derived from a log through sawing or planning (ALSC, 2005)

Medium density fibreboard (MDF): Dry-process fibreboard. When density exceeds 0.8 g/cm³, it may also be referred to as "high-density fibreboard" (HDF) (UNECE *et al.*, 2008)

Monoculture: In general, even-aged, single-species forest crops (BC Ministry of Forests and Range, 2008)

Monitoring: An official ongoing process to verify phytosanitary situations (ISPM No. 05, 2010)

National plant protection organization (NPPO): Official service established by a government to discharge the functions specified by the IPPC (ISPM No. 05, 2010)

Native species (indigenous): A species, subspecies, or lower taxon, occurring within its natural range (past or present) and dispersal potential (i.e. within the range it occupies naturally or could occupy without direct or indirect introduction or care by humans) (IUCN, 2000)

Plants, animals, fungi, and micro-organisms that occur naturally in a given area or region. Synonym: indigenous (UNEP-WCMC, 2010)

See also Indigenous species

Natural enemy: An organism which lives at the expense of another organism in its area of origin and which may help to limit the population of that organism. This includes parasitoids, parasites, predators, phytophagous organisms and pathogens (ISPM No. 05, 2010)

The parasites, parasitoids, predators and pathogens associated in nature with a specific wild population of plants or animals (Dunster and Dunster, 1996)

Naturally regenerated forest: Forest predominantly composed of trees established through natural regeneration (FAO, 2007)

Non-wood forest products: Goods derived from forests that are tangible and physical objects of biological origin other than wood. Generally includes non wood plant and animal products collected from areas defined as forest. Specifically includes the following regardless of whether from natural forests or plantations: gum arabic, rubber/latex and resin; and Christmas trees, cork, bamboo and rattan. Generally excludes products collected in tree stands in agricultural production systems, such as fruit tree plantations, oil palm plantations and agroforestry systems when crops are grown under tree cover. Specifically excludes the following: woody raw materials and products, such as chips, charcoal, fuelwood and wood used for tools, household equipment and carvings; grazing in the forest; and fish and shellfish (FAO, 2007)

Occurrence: The presence in an area of a pest officially recognized to be indigenous or introduced and not officially reported to have been eradicated (ISPM No. 05, 2010)

Organism: Any biotic entity capable of reproduction or replication in its naturally occurring state (ISPM No. 05, 2010)

Oriented strand board (OSB): A structural board in which layers of narrow wafers are layered alternately at right angles in order to give the board greater elastomechanical properties. The wafers, which resemble small pieces of veneer, are coated with e.g. waterproof phenolic resin glue, interleaved together in mats and then bonded together under heat and pressure. The resulting product is a solid, uniform building panel having high strength and water resistance (UNECE *et al.*, 2008)
A structural panel made of narrow strands of fiber oriented lengthwise and crosswise in layers, with a resin binder (Evans, 2000)

Outbreak: A recently detected pest population, including an incursion, or a sudden significant increase of an established pest population in an area (ISPM No. 05, 2010)

Particle board: A panel manufactured from small pieces of wood or other lignocellulosic materials (e.g. chips, flakes, splinters, strands, shreds and shives) bonded together by the use of an organic binder together with one or more of the following agents: heat, pressure, humidity, a catalyst, etc. The particle board category is an aggregate category including oriented strandboard (OSB), waferboard and flaxboard (UNECE *et al.*, 2008)

Pathway: Any means that allows the entry or spread of a pest (ISPM No. 05, 2010)

Pest: Any species, strain or biotype of plant, animal or pathogenic agent injurious to plants or plant products (ISPM No. 05, 2010)
Any organism that is out of place or causes stress to a desired organism (North Carolina State University, 2003)
See also Quarantine pest, Regulated pest, Regulated non-quarantine pest

Pest free area (PFA): An area in which a specific pest does not occur as demonstrated by scientific evidence and in which, where appropriate, this condition is being officially maintained (ISPM No. 05, 2010)

Pest free place of production (PFPP): Place of production in which a specific pest does not occur as demonstrated by scientific evidence and in which, where appropriate, this condition is being officially maintained for a defined period (ISPM No. 05, 2010)

Pest free production site: A defined portion of a place of production in which a specific pest does not occur as demonstrated by scientific evidence and in which, where appropriate, this condition is being officially maintained for a defined period and that is managed as a separate unit in the same way as a pest free place of production (ISPM No. 05, 2010)

Pest risk (for quarantine pests): The probability of introduction and spread of a pest and the magnitude of the associated potential economic consequences (ISPM No. 05, 2010; see Glossary supplement No 2)

Pest risk analysis (PRA): The process of evaluating biological or other scientific and economic evidence to determine whether an organism is a pest, whether it should be regulated, and the strength of any phytosanitary measures to be taken against it (ISPM No. 05, 2010)

Pest risk management (for quarantine pests): Evaluation and selection of options to reduce the risk of introduction and spread of a pest (ISPM No. 05, 2010)

Pest status (in an area): Presence or absence, at the present time, of a pest in an area, including where appropriate its distribution, as officially determined using expert judgment on the basis of current and historical pest records and other information (ISPM No. 05, 2010)

Phytosanitary certificate: Certificate patterned after the model certificates of the IPPC (ISPM No. 05, 2010)

Phytosanitary certification: Use of phytosanitary procedures leading to the issue of a phytosanitary certificate (ISPM No. 05, 2010)

Phytosanitary import requirements: Specific phytosanitary measures established by an importing country concerning consignments moving into that country (ISPM No. 05, 2010)

Phytosanitary measure: Any legislation, regulation or official procedure having the purpose to prevent the introduction and/or spread of quarantine pests, or to limit the economic impact of regulated non-quarantine pests (ISPM No. 05, 2010)

Phytosanitary security (of a consignment): Maintenance of the integrity of a consignment and prevention of its infestation and contamination by regulated pests, through the application of appropriate phytosanitary measures (ISPM No. 05, 2010)

Plant products: Unmanufactured material of plant origin (including grain) and those manufactured products that, by their nature or [by the nature of] their process[ing], may create a risk for the introduction and spread of pests (ISPM No. 05, 2010)

Planted forest: Forest predominantly composed of trees established through planting and/or deliberate seeding (FAO, 2007)

Plants: Living plants and parts thereof, including seeds and germplasm (ISPM No. 05, 2010)

Plant for planting: Plants intended to remain planted, to be planted or replanted (ISPM No. 05, 2010)

Plywood: A panel consisting of an assembly of veneer sheets bonded together with the direction of the grain in alternate plies generally at right angles. The veneer sheets are usually placed symmetrically on both sides of a central ply or core that may itself be made from a veneer sheet or another material. It includes *veneer plywood* (plywood manufactured by bonding together more than two veneer sheets, where the grain of alternate veneer sheets is crossed, generally at right angles); *core plywood* or *blockboard* (plywood with a solid core (i.e. the central layer, generally thicker than the other plies) that consists of narrow boards, blocks or strips of wood placed side by side, which may or may not be glued together); *cellular board* (plywood with a core of cellular construction); and *composite plywood* (plywood with the core or certain layers made of material other than solid wood or veneers) (UNECE *et al.*, 2008)
A flat panel made up of a number of thin sheets or veneers, of wood in which the grain direction of each ply or layer is at right angles to the one adjacent to it. The veneers sheets are united, under pressure, by a bonding agent (Evans, 2000)
Panel products manufactured by gluing together layers of veneer with the grain of alternate of layers oriented at right angles to provide strength (Hubbard *et al.*, 1998)

Provenance: The original geographic source of seed, pollen or propagules. In forestry literature the term is usually considered synonymous with "geographic origin" and preferred to "origin" (FAO/IUFRO, 2002)

Pulp: Commodity class of soft moist mass of wood fiber used in the manufacture of paper. Pulp is made up by reducing wood chips to fibers, either by grinding them up, or by chemical means, and then turning the fibers into slurry (Evans, 2000)

Quarantine pest: A pest of potential economic importance to the area endangered thereby and not yet present there, or present but not widely distributed and being officially controlled (ISPM No. 05, 2010)

Regional plant protection organization (RPPO): An intergovernmental organization with the functions laid down by Article IX of the IPPC (ISPM No. 05, 2010)

Regulated area: An area into which, within which, and/or from which plants, plant products or other regulated articles are subjected to phytosanitary regulations or procedures in order to prevent the introductions and/or spread of quarantine pests or to limit the economic impact of regulated non-quarantine pests (ISPM No. 05, 2010)

Regulated article: Any plant, plant product, storage place, packaging, conveyance, container, soil and any other organism, object or material capable of harbouring or spreading pests, deemed to require phytosanitary measures, particularly where international transportation is involved (ISPM No. 05, 2010)

Regulated non-quarantine pest: A non-quarantine pest whose presence in plants for planting affects the intended use of those plants with an economically unacceptable impact and which is therefore regulated within the territory of the importing contracting party (ISPM No. 05, 2010)

Regulated pest: A quarantine pest or a regulated non-quarantine pest (ISPM No. 05, 2010)

Roundwood: All roundwood felled or otherwise harvested and removed. It comprises all wood obtained from removals, i.e. the quantities removed from forests and from trees outside the forest, including wood recovered from natural, felling and logging losses during the period, calendar year or forest year. It includes all wood removed with or without bark, including wood removed in its round form, or split, roughly squared or in other form (e.g. branches, roots, stumps and burls (where these are harvested) and wood that is roughly shaped or pointed (UNECE *et al.*, 2008)
Wood not sawn longitudinally, carrying its natural rounded surface, with or without bark (ISPM No. 05, 2010)

Sawnwood: Wood that has been produced from both domestic and imported roundwood, either by sawing lengthways or by a profile-chipping process and that, with a few exceptions, exceeds 5 mm in thickness. It includes: planks, beams, joists, boards, rafters, scantlings, laths, boxboards, sleepers and 'lumber', etc., in the following forms: unplaned, planed, grooved, tongued, fingerjointed, chamfered, rabbeted, V-jointed, beaded, etc. (FAO, 2005)
Wood sawn longitudinally, with or without its natural rounded surface with or without bark (ISPM No 5, 2010)

Seeds: A commodity class for seeds for planting or intended for planting and not for consumption or processing (ISPM No. 05, 2010)

Silviculture: The art, science, and practice of establishing, tending, and reproducing forest stands of desired characteristics. It is based on knowledge of species characteristics and environmental requirements (North Carolina State University, 2003)

Species: A population or series of populations of organisms that are capable of interbreeding freely with each other but not with members of other species (FAO/IUFRO, 2002)
See also Indigenous species, Introduced species, Native species

Spread: Expansion of the geographical distribution of a pest within an area (ISPM No. 05, 2010)

Surveillance: An official process which collects and records data on pest occurrence or absence by survey, monitoring or other procedures (ISPM No. 05, 2010)

Survey: An official procedure conducted over a defined period of time to determine the characteristics of a pest population or to determine which species occur in an area (ISPM No. 05, 2010)

Systems approach(es): The integration of different risk management measures, at least two of which act independently, and which cumulatively achieve the appropriate level of protection against regulated pests (ISPM No. 05, 2010)

Technically justified: Justified on the basis of conclusions reached by using an appropriate pest risk analysis or, where applicable, another comparable examination and evaluation of available scientific information (ISPM No. 05, 2010)

Timber: Trees suitable for conversion into industrial forest products. Sometimes this term is used as a synonym for industrial roundwood, and it may also be used to refer to certain large sawn wood products (e.g. bridge timbers) (Dykstra and Heinrich, 1996)

Treatment: Official procedure for the killing, inactivation or removal of pests, or for rendering pests infertile or for devitalization (ISPM No. 05, 2010)

Vector: Literally "a carrier". An animal carrying a micro-organism pathogenic for members of another species; the vector may or may not be essential for the completion of the life cycle of the pathogenic micro-organism (FAO, 2003)
Organisms transmitting pathogens or parasites (FAO, 2010c)
An agent, such as an insect, that may transmit a fungus or other micro-organisms (Tainter and Baker, 1996)

Veneer sheets: Thin sheets of wood of uniform thickness, not exceeding 6 mm, rotary cut (i.e. peeled), sliced or sawn. It includes wood used for the manufacture of laminated construction material, furniture, veneer containers, etc. (UNECE *et al.*, 2008)

Visual examination: The physical examination of plants, plant products, or other regulated articles using the unaided eye, lens, stereoscope or microscope to detect pests or contaminants without testing or processing (ISPM No. 05, 2010)

Voucher specimen or culture: One which acts as a voucher for some specific fact/hypothesis/conclusion, and is, for the fungi typically a dried 'botanical' collection (referred to as a 'gathering' in the International Code of Botanical Nomenclature) or for some taxa a living culture (e.g. yeasts). (McNeill *et al.*, 2006)

Weed: Plant growing where it is not wanted. Generally used to describe plants which colonize readily, and can compete for resources with a planted crop (FAO, 2001)
An aggressive, invasive, easily dispersed plant, one which commonly grows in cultivated ground to the detriment of a crop (van den Bosch, Messenger and Gutierrez, 1981)

Wood: A commodity class for round wood, sawn wood, wood chips or dunnage, with or without bark (ISPM No. 05, 2010)

Woodfuel: Wood from forests, shrubs and other trees used as fuel. Woodfuels can be divided into four types of products: fuelwood, charcoal, black liquor and other (i.e. methanol, ethanol, pyrolitic gas) (FAO, 2004)

Wood-based panels: A product category that is an aggregate comprising veneer sheets, plywood, particle board and fibreboard (UNECE *et al.*, 2008)

Wood chips: Chipped woody biomass in the form of pieces with a defined particle size produced by mechanical treatment with sharp tools such as knives. Wood chips have a subrectangular shape with a typical length 5 to 50 mm and a low thickness compared to other dimensions (FAO, 2004)
Wood that has been reduced to small pieces and is suitable for pulping, for particle board and/or fibreboard production, for use as a fuel, or for other purposes (UNECE *et al.*, 2008)
Wood fragments broken or shredded from any wood (APHIS, 2010)

Wood mulch: Bark chips, wood chips, wood shavings, or sawdust intended for use as a protective or decorative ground cover (APHIS, 2010)

Wood packaging materials: Wood or wood products (excluding paper products) used in supporting, protecting or carrying a commodity (includes dunnage) (ISPM No. 05, 2010)

Annex 3

International Standards for Phytosanitary Measures (ISPMs)

A brief description of the adopted ISPMs is provided below. The full text of the ISPMs can be found on the IPPC Web site at: www.ippc.int (Core activities – Adopted Standards). ISPMs are published in Arabic, Chinese, English, French, Russian and Spanish. This list is current as of December 2010.

ISPM No. 01 (2006), *Phytosanitary principles for the protection of plants and the application of phytosanitary measures in international trade*
This standard describes basic phytosanitary principles related to plant protection including those related to the application of phytosanitary measures to the international movement of people, commodities and conveyances, as well as those related to the objectives of the IPPC.

ISPM No. 02 (2007), *Framework for pest risk analysis*
This standard describes the pest risk analysis (PRA) process within the scope of the IPPC and introduces the three stages of pest risk analysis – initiation, pest risk assessment and pest risk management. The standard focuses on the initiation stage. Generic issues of information gathering, documentation, risk communication, uncertainty and consistency are also considered.

ISPM No. 03 (2005), *Guidelines for the export, shipment, import and release of biological control agents and other beneficial organisms*
This standard provides guidelines for risk management related to the export, transportation, import and release of beneficial organisms. It describes the related responsibilities of contracting parties to the IPPC, NPPOs or other responsible authorities, importers and exporters. The standard considers biological control agents capable of self-replication (including parasitoids, predators, parasites, nematodes, phytophagous organisms, and pathogens such as fungi, bacteria and viruses), as well as sterile insects and other beneficial organisms (such as mycorrhizae and pollinators), and includes those packaged or formulated as commercial products. Provisions are also included for import for research in quarantine facilities of non-indigenous biological control agents and other beneficial organisms. This standard does not include living modified organisms, issues related to the registration of biopesticides, or microbial agents intended for vertebrate pest control.

ISPM No. 04 (1995), *Requirements for the establishment of Pest Free Areas*
This standard describes the requirements for the establishment and use of pest free areas (PFAs) as a risk management option for phytosanitary certification of plants, plant products and other regulated articles exported from the PFA or to support the scientific justification for phytosanitary measures taken by an importing country for protection of an endangered PFA.

ISPM No. 05 (2010), *Glossary of phytosanitary terms*
This reference standard is a list of terms and definitions with specific meaning for phytosanitary systems worldwide. It has been developed to provide a harmonized internationally agreed vocabulary associated with the implementation of the IPPC and ISPMs and is being regularly revised.

ISPM No. 06 (1997), *Guidelines for surveillance*
This standard describes general surveillance and specific surveys, and specifies the components of survey and monitoring systems for the purpose of pest detection and the supply of information for use in pest risk analyses, the establishment of pest free areas and, where appropriate, the preparation of pest lists.

ISPM No. 07 (1997), *Export certification system*
This standard describes the components of a national system of procedures leading to the issuance of phytosanitary certificates.

ISPM No. 08 (1998), *Determination of pest status in an area*
This standard describes the content of a pest record, and the use of pest records and other information in the determination of pest status in an area. Descriptions of pest status categories are provided as well as recommendations for good reporting practices.

ISPM No. 09 (1998), *Guidelines for pest eradication programmes*
This standard describes the components of a pest eradication programme which can lead to the establishment or re-establishment of pest absence in an area.

ISPM No. 10 (1999), *Requirements for the establishment of pest free places of production and pest free production sites*
This standard describes the requirements for the establishment and use of pest free places of production and pest free production sites as pest risk management options for meeting phytosanitary requirements for the import of plants, plant products and other regulated articles.

ISPM No. 11 (2004), *Pest risk analysis for quarantine pests including analysis of environmental risks and living modified organisms*
This standard provides details for the use of pest risk analysis (PRA) to determine if pests qualify as quarantine pests and describes the processes to be used for risk

assessment and selection of pest risk management options. It also includes details regarding the analysis of risks of plant pests to the environment and biological diversity, including those risks affecting uncultivated and unmanaged plants, wild flora, habitats and ecosystems contained in the PRA area. It also includes guidance on evaluating the potential phytosanitary risks to plants and plant products posed by living modified organisms (LMOs).

ISPM No. 12 (2001), *Guidelines for phytosanitary certificates*
This standard describes principles and guidelines for the preparation and issue of phytosanitary certificates and phytosanitary certificates for re-export.

ISPM No. 13 (2001), *Guidelines for the notification of non-compliance and emergency action*
This standard describes the actions to be taken by countries regarding the notification of non-compliance of a consignment with phytosanitary import requirements including the detection of specified regulated pests. In addition it outlines when and how an emergency action should be taken when there is a detection of a regulated pest or an organism which may pose a potential phytosanitary threat.

ISPM No. 14 (2002), *The use of integrated measures in a systems approach for pest risk management*
This standard provides guidelines for the development and evaluation of integrated measures in a systems approach as an option for pest risk management.

ISPM No. 15 (2009), *Regulation of wood packaging material in international trade*
This standard describes phytosanitary measures that reduce the risk of introduction and spread of quarantine pests associated with the movement in international trade of wood packaging material made from raw wood. Wood packaging material covered by this standard includes dunnage, but excludes wood packaging made from wood which does not exceed 6mm thickness or processed in such a way that it is free from pests (i.e. plywood).

ISPM No. 16 (2002), *Regulated non-quarantine pests: concept and application*
This standard describes the concept of regulated non-quarantine pests associated with plants for planting and identifies their characteristics. The standard describes the application and the relevant elements for regulatory systems.

ISPM No. 17 (2002), *Pest reporting*
This standard describes the responsibilities of and requirements for contracting parties to the IPPC in reporting the occurrence, outbreak or spread of pests in areas for which they are responsible. It also provides guidance on reporting successful eradication of pests and establishment of pest free areas.

ISPM No. 18 (2003), *Guidelines for the use of irradiation as a phytosanitary measure*

This standard provides technical guidance on the specific procedures for the application of ionizing radiation as a phytosanitary treatment for regulated pests or articles. This does not include treatments used for: the production of sterile organisms for pest control; sanitary treatments (food safety and animal health); the preservation or improvement of commodity quality (i.e., shelf life extension); or inducing mutagenesis.

ISPM No. 19 (2003), *Guidelines on lists of regulated pests*

This standard describes the procedures to develop, maintain and make available national lists of regulated pests.

ISPM No. 20 (2004), *Guidelines for a phytosanitary import regulatory system*

This standard describes the structure and operation of a phytosanitary import regulatory system and the rights, obligations and responsibilities which should be considered in establishing, operating and revising such a system.

ISPM No. 21 (2004), *Pest risk analysis for regulated non quarantine pests*

This standard provides guidelines for conducting pest risk analysis for regulated non-quarantine pests (RNQPs). It describes the integrated processes to be used for risk assessment and the selection of risk management options to achieve a specified pest tolerance level.

ISPM No. 22 (2005), *Requirements for the establishment of areas of low pest prevalence*

This standard describes the requirements and procedures for the establishment of Areas of Low Pest Prevalence (ALPP) for regulated pests in an area, and to facilitate export of a commodity, where pests are regulated by an importing country. This includes the identification, verification, maintenance and use of ALPPs.

ISPM No. 23 (2005), *Guidelines for inspection*

This standard describes procedures for the inspection of consignments of plants, plant products and other regulated articles at import and export. It is focused on the determination of consignment compliance with phytosanitary requirements, based on visual examination, documentary checks, and identity and integrity checks.

ISPM No. 24 (2005), *Guidelines for the determination and recognition of equivalence of phytosanitary measures*

This standard describes the principles and requirements related to the determination and recognition of equivalence of phytosanitary measures. It also describes a procedure for equivalence determinations in international trade.

ISPM No. 25 (2006), *Consignments in transit*
This standard describes procedures to identify, assess and manage phytosanitary risks associated with consignments of regulated articles which pass through a country without being imported, in such a manner that any phytosanitary measures applied in the country of transit are technically justified and necessary to prevent the introduction into and/or spread of pests within that country.

ISPM No. 26 (2006), *Establishment of pest free areas for fruit flies (Tephritidae)*
This standard provides guidelines for the establishment of pest free areas for fruit flies of economic importance, and for the maintenance of their pest free status.

ISPM No. 27 (2006), *Diagnostic protocols for regulated pests*
This standard provides guidance on the structure and content of the IPPC diagnostic protocols for regulated pests. The protocols describe procedures and methods for the official diagnosis of regulated pests that are relevant for international trade. They provide at least the minimum requirements for reliable diagnosis of regulated pests. As diagnostic protocols for regulated pests are adopted by the CPM they will be annexed to this standard.

ISPM No. 28 (2009), *Phytosanitary treatments for regulated pests*
This standard describes the requirements for submission and evaluation of the efficacy data and other relevant information on a phytosanitary treatment that can be used as a phytosanitary measure for the control of regulated pests on regulated articles, primarily those moving in international trade. The adopted treatments provide the minimum requirements necessary to control a regulated pest at a stated efficacy. As phytosanitary treatments are adopted by the CPM they will be annexed to this standard.

ISPM No. 29 (2007), *Recognition of pest free areas and areas of low pest prevalence*
This standard provides guidance and describes a procedure for the bilateral recognition of pest free areas and areas of low pest prevalence. It also provides some considerations regarding pest free places of production and pest free production sites.

ISPM No. 30 (2008), *Establishment of areas of low pest prevalence for fruit flies (Tephritidae)*
This standard provides guidelines for the establishment and maintenance of areas of low pest prevalence for fruit flies by an NPPO. These areas may be utilized as official pest risk management measures alone, or as part of a systems approach.

ISPM No. 31 (2008), *Methodologies for sampling of consignments*
This standard provides guidance to NPPOs in selecting appropriate sampling methodologies (based and not based on statistics) for inspection or testing of

consignments to verify compliance with phytosanitary requirements. It also provides guidance on the definition of an appropriate sample size. This standard does not give guidance on field sampling (for example, as required for surveys).

ISPM No. 32 (2009), *Categorization of commodities according to their pest risk*
This standard provides criteria for NPPOs of importing countries on how to categorize commodities according to their pest risk when considering import requirements. This categorization should help in identifying whether further pest risk analysis is required and if phytosanitary certification is needed.
The first stage of categorization is based on whether the commodity has been processed and, if so, the method and degree of processing to which the commodity has been subjected before export. The second stage of categorization of commodities is based on their intended use after import. Contaminating pests or storage pests that may become associated with the commodity after processing are not considered in this standard.

ISPM No. 33 (2010), *Pest free potato (***Solanum*** spp.) micropropagative material and minitubers for international trade*
This standard provides guidance on the production, maintenance and phytosanitary certification of pest free potato (*Solanum tuberosum* and related tuber-forming species) micropropagative material and minitubers intended for international trade. It does not apply to field-grown propagative material of potato or to potatoes intended for consumption or processing.

ISPM No. 34 (2010), *Design and operation of post-entry quarantine stations for plants*
This standard describes general guidelines for the design and operation of post-entry quarantine (PEQ) stations for holding imported consignments of plants, mainly plants for planting, in confinement in order to verify whether or not they are infested with quarantine pests.

Annex 4
Where to go for more information

FAO
FAO Forest Health: www.fao.org/forestry/pests/en
FAO Invasive Species: www.fao.org/forestry/aliens/en
Biosecurity in forestry: www.fao.org/forestry/biosecurity/
FAO Priority Area for Inter-disciplinary Action – Biosecurity for agriculture and food production: www.fao.org/biosecurity
FAO/WHO Codex Alimentarius Commission: www.codexalimentarius.net
North American Forestry Commission, Exotic Pest Information System for North America (EXFOR) – http://spfnic.fs.fed.us/exfor

Other international and regional organizations, conventions and information portals
Australian Weed Risk Assessment: www.weeds.org.au/riskassessment.htm
CabAbstracts: www.cabdirect.org
CABI Forestry Compendium: www.cabi.org/fc
Convention on Biological Diversity (CBD): www.cbd.int
Convention on International Trade in Endangered Species of Wild Fauna and Flora (CITES): www.cites.org/eng/disc/species.shtml
Commission on Sustainable Development (CSD): www.un.org/esa/dsd/csd/csd_aboucsd.shtml
Delivering Alien Invasive Species Inventories for Europe: www.europe-aliens.org
Global Invasive Species Programme (GISP): www.gisp.org
Global Invasive Species Database: www.issg.org/database
International Plant Protection Convention (IPPC): www.ippc.int
International Portal on Food Safety, Animal and Plant Health (IPFSAPH): www.ipfsaph.org
International Union for Conservation of Nature (IUCN)/SSC Invasive Species Specialist Group (ISSG): www.issg.org
International Union of Forest Research Organizations (IUFRO) Unit 7.03.12 – Alien invasive species and international trade: www.iufro.org/science/divisions/division-7
North European and Baltic Network on Invasive Alien Species (NOBANIS): www.nobanis.org
World Trade Organization (WTO): www.wto.org
World Trade Organization (WTO) Sanitary and Phytosanitary Measures (SPS): www.wto.org/english/tratop_e/sps_e/sps_e.htm

FAO FORESTRY PAPERS

Availability: February 2011

Ar	–	Arabic	Multil	–	Multilingual
C	–	Chinese	*	–	Out of print
E	–	English			
I	–	Italian			
F	–	French			
P	–	Portuguese			
S	–	Spanish			
R	–	Russian			

The FAO Technical Papers are available through the authorized FAO Sales Agents or directly from Sales and Marketing Group, FAO, Viale delle Terme di Caracalla, 00153 Rome, Italy.